The Foodie Handbook

The Foodie Handbook
The (Almost) Definitive Guide to Gastronomy

by Pim Techamuanvivit

Color photography by Pim Techamuanvivit
Black-and-white photography by Jenny Acheson

CHRONICLE BOOKS
SAN FRANCISCO

How to love food (again)

Relationships that matter most in our lives are often complicated. Think of the one with your mother or your current love, and, perhaps the most perplexing, food. These liaisons can be fraught with love, hate, joy, fear, trust, suspicion, and a whole host of other emotions. Sometimes it is nearly enough to make us wish we were orphans, turn us celibate or, worse yet, vegan.

You can see it in the confounding way we describe food: a chocolate cake is decadent and sinfully delicious, pictures of food that tickle your mouth to water are food porn, simple dishes many of us enjoy are dismissed as merely comfort food, while intricate cuisine composed of exquisite ingredients is pretentious or haughty – fit to eat only with a sneer (at those unworthy to share such indulgence) and perhaps with a pinkie or two extended. It seems almost impossible to say anything at all about food without a pang of regret, without apologizing for some sort of offense, real or imagined. No wonder food is such a lost cause to so many.

You can even see it in the way a recipe is written. On one side, quickie recipes filled with shortcuts and trickeries claim to liberate you from the debilitating shackles of cooking to feed yourself and your family. Just add water and the "lunch-o-matic" does the rest! On the other side, the "real food" movements admonish us, as though the demands of our fast-paced lives should register not at all, to do things the slowest and most difficult (and often most expensive) way possible (not unlike the sentence you are reading).

What is easily lost in all of this is the simple love of food, that rush of joy when you taste something truly delicious. You remember a moment like that still, yes? Perhaps that summer when you were eight, standing near an ice cream vendor in the park on a hot afternoon, a cone in your hand. Most of the yummy chocolate ice cream had probably melted, dripping halfway down to your elbow, but you hardly cared. Back when your love of food was, simply, pure joy, all your attention was focused on that sweet, creamy, chocolaty deliciousness you were savoring. This was back before you even knew what the word *savoring* meant, but you savored it anyway. Way back, before that simple act of eating an ice cream cone became tainted with a hint of fear of that extra inch it could add to your waistline, or what dubious chemicals may lurk in that creamy goodness. Don't you wish your food life was that simple still?

Call me a dreamer, but I believe we can get back there. Just as we deal with other relationships in our life, sometimes it pays to gloss over some issues and focus on what makes us happy. It won't make the difficult issues go away, but it might let us enjoy things a bit more. It might even inspire us to work out some of those issues when we can. We could deal with our life of food realistically rather than ideally, and take a few shortcuts when we need to without feeling like we are somehow cheating. Enjoy something exquisite without apologizing for the indulgence. Or think about how to eat responsibly – for our own body as well as for our planet – without having it be a preoccupation, just so we can still enjoy a Kit Kat bar now and again without the guilt.

Talking about the foods that bring us joy and learning how to eat better while having fun is exactly what I envisioned for this book. **The first step to being a real foodie is learning to love food again. Do you still have it in you?**

1 | How to eat like a foodie

Taste like a foodie

Eternal optimists believe there is innate goodness in everyone's heart. I'm a foodie optimist. I believe there's an innate sense of good taste in everyone, an inner foodie, if you must. Give someone a perfect peach to taste and they will know it, if only they take a moment to savor it.

A box of battered and deep-fried nuggets of chicken sums up what is wrong with food today. The protein itself is of questionable provenance: where on a chicken is a nugget exactly? Don't you find it odd that in a world full of things that apparently taste like chicken, those nuggets manage to taste not the least bit like one? Not helping matters is a choice of sickly sweet sauces of dubious ethnic origins that accompany them, each tasting of nothing much more than sugar, salt, and fake flavorings.

Junk foods like these don't exactly taste bad, mind you. They are precisely designed – engineered even – to appeal to the most primal of our gustatory desires: the need for fat and sugar as efficient sources of calories, and for sodium chloride, a mineral crucial to the mechanics of our bodies. Some people think junk food tastes kind of good. I suspect they are the same people who think a tracksuit is appropriate attire for a nice day out.

It's time we stop letting ourselves be fooled into thinking that junk foods taste good; our brains are being tricked into believing that such foods are giving us what we need. It's high time we tasted real food, explored the rich, diverse world of flavors, and liberate our taste buds. It's time we let out our inner foodie.

Foods with deep, complex flavors are not always complicated to make. Here are three recipes that are delightfully simple, showcasing the bright, clear flavor of each ingredient. Unlike the many processed foods that taste merely vaguely of something or other, here, you will know exactly what you are eating. You will also be astonished by the complex deliciousness that these deceptively simple ingredients and flavors can create. Do try them. Taste like a foodie.

Strawberries in hibiscus and vanilla soup
Recipe adapted from Alain Passard

Alain Passard serves this dessert at his three-star restaurant L'Arpège in Paris. The mélange of flavors is so unique that you might find it suspect, until you taste it. Instead of muddling the flavors, the genius of this recipe is in how each taste not only remains unique but also accentuates the other flavors so that each tastes more like itself. The hint of floral hibiscus deepens and concentrates the fruity strawberries. The vanilla and sugar tame the astringent hibiscus, keeping it assertive yet never aggressive. This dessert is a true delight that you must try. How good can this simple recipe be, you ask? I once received a marriage proposal from someone I made this for. I suggested he take it to Alain Passard himself.

SERVES 6

2 cups | 500ml water
³/4 cup | 150g sugar
1 vanilla pod (or, substitute with ¹/2 teaspoon of vanilla extract in a pinch)
1 cup | 25g dry hibiscus flowers (also called Jamaica flowers)
2 pints | 500g strawberries, hulled and quartered

TO SERVE: *Vanilla ice cream & a shot of Caribbean rum (optional)*

Place the water and sugar in a small saucepan and bring to a boil. Lower the heat to simmer and continue to cook for 5 minutes. Turn off the heat.
 Cut the vanilla pod lengthwise with a knife. Using the tip of the knife, dull-side down, scrape the pod from one end to the other to

remove the tiny black seeds. Add the seeds and the vanilla pod halves (or the vanilla extract, if using) to the water and sugar mixture. Then add the dry hibiscus flowers and stir well. Let the syrup macerate with the vanilla and hibiscus until it cools down completely.

Place the strawberries in a bowl large enough to contain them and the syrup – and pretty enough for the table. Cover the top with plastic wrap and refrigerate until ready to use.

Once the hibiscus syrup has cooled down completely, strain it into another bowl. Discard the hibiscus flowers and vanilla pod halves, cover the bowl with plastic wrap and set aside to cool in the fridge.

One hour before serving, pour the hibiscus and vanilla syrup over the strawberries and mix gently. Cover with plastic wrap and return to the fridge until serving. Don't let the berries soak in the syrup for much longer than an hour or they will begin to soften and break down.

Serve the berries by themselves or over a scoop or two of good vanilla ice cream. A shot of rum in it will do just fine, too – something good, and perhaps with a bit of age.

Warm apricots with honey and saffron
Recipe adapted from Ferran Adrià

Here is another inspired combination of flavors that will win you praises at your next dinner party. It will win you even bigger praises when you tell your guests that the recipe idea came from the wizard of modern Spanish cuisine Ferran Adrià whose restaurant elBulli is the toughest reservation in the world. Combining flavors so diverse and unexpected as apricot and saffron is Ferran's signature. Here, the warm apricots – even the bland ones from early in the season – take on a deeper flavor, accentuated by the fragrant honey. The saffron adds a savory restraint to the dish, keeping it safely away from cloying sweetness. Ingenious.

Continued

1lb | 450g apricots
1 vanilla bean pod
4 tablespoons honey (the darkest you can find)
a small pinch of saffron

TO SERVE: *Vanilla ice cream (optional)*
PREHEAT THE OVEN TO: *400°F | 200°C | Gas Mark 6*

Cut the apricots in half, following the indentation on the skin and cutting around the pit. Discard the pits and arrange the apricot halves, skin-side down, in a baking dish large enough to contain all the apricots in one layer.

Cut the vanilla pod lengthwise with a knife. Using the tip of the knife, dull-side down, scrape the pod from one end to the other to remove the tiny black seeds. Dip the tip of your finger on the vanilla seeds and smear a little bit on the cut side of each apricot. Drizzle the honey over the apricot halves. Pick up the saffron strands, crumbling them between your fingers a bit to break them into smaller strands. Sprinkle them over the apricot halves, making sure you spread the saffron evenly. When in doubt, use a little less. Saffron is quite heady and might overpower the other flavors in the dish if too much is used.

Place the baking dish in the preheated oven and bake for 12 minutes. Remove from the oven and let cool for a few minutes before serving. These baked apricots will taste best when warm – not piping hot. Serve by themselves or with vanilla ice cream.

Simple bread and onion soup

This soup contains three main ingredients: bread, onions and milk. When you taste it, you might not believe the extraordinarily complex and creamy soup these three simple ingredients produce. The key is to coax each ingredient to express its primal quality. The onions are cooked slowly until they are reduced to its core onion-ness. The bread – preferably from a delicious country loaf – is toasted to add yet another dimension of flavor. The milk and bread combine to create a silky smooth texture, adding richness to the already flavorful soup.

Continued

1¹/₂ cups | 70g stale bread, cut into 1-inch/2.5-cm cubes
3 cups | 750ml milk
1 tablespoon butter or olive oil
3 cups | 350g thinly sliced onions
1 cup | 250ml water
¹/₂ to 1 tablespoon salt
black pepper

TO GARNISH: *Dollop of crème fraîche and a sprinkling of finely chopped chives*
EQUIPMENT: *Regular blender or an immersion blender*

Toast the bread cubes until brown on all sides in a toaster oven, or simply toss them in a pan over medium heat. When the bread cubes are well browned, transfer them to a medium-sized bowl and pour in the milk. Set aside to soak while you cook the onions.

Melt the butter in a large frying pan over low to medium heat. Add the onion slices and stir occasionally for about 20 to 30 minutes. The goal is to caramelize the onions but not burn them. If the pan gets too hot and the onions begin to burn quickly, sprinkle a bit of water over them, lower the heat, and continue to cook until they are well caramelized.

When the onions are done, add them, with the milk and bread, to a medium saucepan. (If you plan to use an immersion blender to blend the soup later, make sure you use a large saucepan so the content does not spill over when blending.) Add the water, half a tablespoon of salt, two turns of the peppermill and cook over medium heat until boiling. Lower the heat to simmer and let it cook for 3 to 5 minutes, until the bread cubes are completely soft.

Blend the content until smooth, with an immersion blender directly in the pan, or transfer the content into a regular stand blender. (If using the regular stand blender, once the soup is smooth pour it back into the pan.) Check the seasonings and add more salt or pepper as needed. If you find the soup on the sweet side from the caramelized onions, add a bit more salt to correct it.

Serve the soup in a bowl or a cute coffee mug. Just before serving, drop in a dollop of crème fraîche and sprinkle over finely chopped chives.

Dine like a foodie
Or how to get the best out of a three-star experience

Don't you feel it? Entering the room at a three-star restaurant, sneaking glances at the impeccably dressed people around you, don't you feel that everyone is in on some kind of secret? They don't appear to have trouble understanding each other, but for all you know they are speaking in tongues. Everybody knows the cue, what to do, how to hold themselves, which fork (not) to use on the white asparagus and Osetra caviar. Waiters, diners, and sommeliers traverse the room in varying tempo yet in perfect harmony. The entire restaurant scene is a well choreographed dance – and you somehow missed the rehearsal. Now you are a beat behind and always in danger of squishing someone else's toes. Worse yet, you are shelling out big money for this privilege.

You don't really need me to point out that this is, of course, all in your head. It's still no less intimidating though, and you know that, too. Fret not my friends. Help has arrived. This survival guide will help you not only stay alive but the make the best out of this experience.

First of all, you need an attitude adjustment. This party is in your honor, baby. You are not the one who should be intimidated. You're the guest of honor at table and, more important, you're the one holding the purse. This is your dining experience. The staff at the restaurant is there to make it a wonderful time. They are there to help you.

Okay, before you take this too far, by no means am I giving you carte blanche to order people around for kicks. Some people do that in hope of establishing a kind of order or hierarchy, showing off who is king in this castle. That they are the one most intimidated is, sadly, often transparent to all but the blustering diners themselves. Other diners act out in this way as a kind of armor against all manners of imagined offenses, such as being served a lesser cut of meat or an inferior piece of fish, or being coerced into an over-priced bottle of wine. Alas, these pre-emptive strikes do not guarantee a great experience – quite often they achieve exactly the opposite.

Going to a restaurant is not entering a battleground where either the smart diner or the wily house must win in the end. Instead, think of your restaurant visit as an act of collaboration, with the chef, the dining room staff, and you, working in blissful harmony to create the best possible experience for everyone. You think I am sporting a pair of rose-colored glasses. You might even be right, but the way I see it is this: there are good, honest restaurants, and then there are bad restaurants. If you happen to find yourself in a treacherous restaurant – intent on cheating you out of as much money as they possibly could – no amount of bullying will make them honest. The best course of action for you is never to return. On the other hand, if you are at a different kind of restaurant, whose goal is to give the customers a superlative experience (which, in my opinion, is the case in most great restaurants anywhere in the world) all the browbeating will only turn the staff bitter and backfire on you.

In my experience, restaurant staff appreciates diners who are courteous, curious, and eager to experience something new. They delight in guiding the guests through the menu and the wine list. It's the know-it-all diners upon whom everyone frowns and even sneers at behind their backs. I once found myself sitting next to one such diner, who insisted that he understood enough French for him not to need any assistance with the menu. As his main course he chose something he thought was veal. I saw the waiter trying to chime in to explain something, but the indignant diner dismissively brushed the waiter aside. And what do you know? The dish turned out to be *rognon de veau*, veal kidney, perfectly seared and presented in a shiny copper pan. I could tell he really didn't like the dish (*rognon de veau* being something of an acquired taste) but, too proud to admit his blunder, he had to muster through, pretending he knew what he had ordered all along.

At the very high end of restaurants, chefs fashion themselves artists and master artisans, with strong styles and a clearly defined

HOW TO EAT LIKE A FOODIE

philosophy of cuisine. In this case it's probably worth it to let them take the lead. It's like going to a dance. Have you ever danced with someone who's really good? Think Al Pacino in *Scent of a Woman*. Dancing with someone that good elevates you to a whole new level. You just have to close your eyes and let yourself be led.

No. I'm not asking you to give up all control. In the end, you are the one who has to eat the food. So, by all means, be clear about what you like and don't like, and do tell the kitchen about it. I, for one, dislike beetroot. Actually, *dislike* is far too mild a word. Perhaps a better fit would be *detest, abhor, loathe, abominate* – I could go on. Every time I go to Arpège in Paris I get into the same discussion with the servers:

"But it's chef's speciality," they argue.

"I don't care. I do not eat beetroot." I say.

"But… but," they protest.

It all ends the same way. Even Alain Passard cannot make a beetroot dish that I will eat. I stand my ground, and so should you. To get the best out of your restaurant experience, here are some basic rules:

Plan ahead It never hurts to learn something about a restaurant before you go. Read about the chef and his or her style of cooking. Find out the speciality on the menu and on the wine list. There are plenty of resources at your fingertips, from food boards, blogs, and online newspaper archives. Google is your friend. Google them.

Make your reservation well in advance. Even your rich, well connected friends cannot be trusted to pull a tough reservation out of their, um, *hat*, every time, so plan ahead. For a reservation in a different country send a fax or e-mail. This is better than leaving a garbled message on an answering machine in a language that the reservationists might have difficulty understanding. Make sure you get a confirmation e-mail or fax before jumping on a plane. If you don't hear back within a week, then call them.

Cultivate your relationships If you plan to go back to that restaurant again, make sure it is your name on the reservation book. Great restaurants keep meticulous records of their patrons. You can almost guarantee a better, warmer reception with each return visit. Before long, it will be you who could pull a tough reservation out of your hat for your desperate friends.

Give the restaurant a courtesy warning If you or anyone in your party has dietary restrictions, be sure to inform the restaurant when you make the reservation. Any great restaurant will be happy to accommodate special requests, but it is a courtesy to let them know beforehand. I once helped a friend host a fancy dinner for 90 diners, cooked by a famous chef at a local farm. A pair of guests showed up on the day of the dinner, which was being cooked in a makeshift kitchen out in the field somewhere, and told us that they were vegetarians and would require a fully animal-free meal. It took all I had in me not to hand them each a pair of kitchen shears and tell them to go forage their own food in the field, right over there. Regular restaurant kitchens will be better equipped to deal with this than our campfire kitchen that day, but it is still a courtesy to allow them to prepare for it. Chances are you will get better food at the end of this bargain as well.

Make friends with the restaurant staff I read somewhere that a great restaurant meal is a conspiracy between the diner, waiter, and chef. And what you should certainly avoid is the kind of conspiracy that has the chef and service staff plotting against you.

It is to your advantage to be courteous to everyone, from the maître d'hotel to the guy clearing your soup plate off the table. Be respectful of the chef. Bring them all into your team. Get them to be in your conspiracy. Don't force them to plot one against you.

Keep it local Most great restaurants take pride in showcasing special products from their region. Don't go to Maison de Bricourt in Brittany and order a steak – that's not what they are about. The chef, Olivier Roellinger, makes magic with superlative local seafood and young *pré salé* lamb from the nearby salt marshes. At the restaurant Michel Bras in Laguiole in the wilds of the Aubrac in southwest France, the chef roams the surrounding hills in search of herbs and wild greens for his famous salad "Gargouillou." Ordering dishes featuring local ingredients is a great way to acknowledge the chef's specialities and pay respect to the restaurant's roots.

Think seasonal Besides using local ingredients to create a sense of place – connecting the restaurant to its unique surroundings – great restaurants also highlight prime ingredients and preparations in harmony with the changing seasons. This keeps the diners interested and the chef engaged and constantly evolving, a way of propelling already lofty restaurants to even greater heights. Be wary of restaurants where the menu never changes. I often run the other way when I see truffles featured in a year-round menu of a restaurant. To me it indicates static, unimaginative chefs relying on luxury ingredients to create an expensive menu. I have no interest at all in eating winter truffles in summer. They are mediocre at best, and more often propelled to even deeper mediocrity by the addition of gnarly truffle oil. Faux luxury ingredients are the nouveau riche of gastronomy.

You should be able to learn which local ingredients are in season by doing a bit of research in advance. If not, the restaurant staff should be more than happy to guide you. Keeping it local works very well for navigating wine lists as well. Don't order a bottle of Claret in Burgundy. It's probably not the best deal on the list.

Don't be bashful Ask questions. Don't be shy. Showing them that you are curious will always work better than pretending to be a know-it-all.

Tell them what you want and don't be hesitant about it. If you prefer your meat well-done, no one should stop you ordering it that way. In the end it's your food and your digestive system. That said, if your dietary restrictions run to two pages long, it might be best to stay in and eat at home.

The sommelier doesn't know what you want to drink Asking a sommelier to make your wine selection for you can result in a multitude of nasty surprises. Not that I think sommeliers are out to get us, but simply asking them to "pick something" is not giving them much to work with. From my experience, very few sommeliers are clairvoyant. Give them some ideas about the style of wine you like, perhaps some bottles you've enjoyed, and also give them a price point as a guide. A good sommelier should be delighted to work with you this way.

When all else fails, let out your inner empress At times, despite our best intentions and manners, we still encounter restaurant staff with the attitude of an insufferable snob. We've all been through this at one time or another. When all else fails, in a case like this, I suggest you let out your inner empress.

Have you seen the movie *The Last Emperor*? Do you remember that empress-mother? She was the little old lady who was carried around everywhere in a sedan, and who, in one scene, sat on a great big golden throne being served turtle soup from a cauldron the size of a wading pool, with a giant live turtle simmering slowly in it. Yes, that one. She's hiding somewhere inside each and every one of us, and this is the time to let her out.

I must warn you, this revenge is best served with impeccable manners and a beguiling smile. Remember, again, that this is your show. You are the star, so act like one. Tell them your water has too much ice, and to please take a few cubes away. Or mention that your knife has a spot, so minuscule perhaps you are the only one who saw it, but they should replace it just the same. Ask detailed questions about a dish, especially if it means sending the waiters back to the kitchen repeatedly to "confirm with the chef." Order something, then change your mind, and perhaps again, but remember, do it all with impeccable manners. Playing a snob is a power game. I don't advise you to start one, but if someone else does, it is you who will win every time.

Synthesis of elBulli cuisine

1. Cooking is a language through which all the following properties may be expressed: harmony, creativity, happiness, beauty, poetry, complexity, magic, humor, provocation and culture.

2. The use of top quality products and technical knowledge to prepare them properly are taken for granted.

3. All products have the same gastronomic value, regardless of their price.

4. Preference is given to vegetables and seafood, with a key role also being played by dairy products, nuts and other products that make up a light form of cooking. In recent years red meat and large cuts of poultry have been very sparingly used.

5. Although the characteristics of the products may be modified (temperature, texture, shape, etc.), the aim is always to preserve the purity of their original flavor, except for processes that call for long cooking or seek the nuances of particular reactions such as the Maillard reaction.

6. Cooking techniques, both classic and modern, are a heritage that the cook has to know how to exploit to the maximum.

7. As has occurred in most fields of human evolution down the ages, new technologies are a resource for the progress of cooking.

8. The family of stocks is being extended. Together with the classic ones, lighter stocks performing an identical function are now being used (waters, broths, consommés, clarified vegetable juices, nut milk, etc.).

9. The information given off by a dish is enjoyed through the senses; it is also enjoyed and interpreted by reflection.

10. Taste is not the only sense that can be stimulated: touch can also be played with (contrasts of temperatures and textures), as well as smell, sight (colors, shapes, trompe d'oeil, etc.), whereby the five senses become one of the main points of reference in the creative cooking process.

11. The technique - concept search is the apex of the creative pyramid.

12. Creation involves teamwork. In addition, research has become consolidated as a new feature of the culinary creative process.

13. The barriers between the sweet and savory world are being broken down. Importance is being given to a new cold cuisine, particularly in the creation of the frozen savory world.

14. The classical structure of dishes is being broken down: a veritable revolution is underway in first courses and desserts, closely bound up with the concept of symbiosis between the sweet and savory world; in main dishes the "product-garnish-sauce" hierarchy is being broken down.

15. A new way of serving food is being promoted. The dishes are finished in the dining room by the serving staff. In other cases the diners themselves participate in this process.

16. Regional cuisine as a style is an expression of its own geographical and cultural context as well as its culinary traditions. Its bond with nature complements and enriches th

17. Products and other countries are subjected to one's particular style

18. There ar aining harmony of products and flavors: through ional cooking traditions, adaptation, deconst s), or through new combinations.

19. A culinar which is becoming more and more ordered, tha nes a relationship with the world and langua

ony is to be found in small

ance are completely legitind to, or are closely bound

sion of avant - garde cooking. oncepts such as snacks, to their own.

s from different fields etc.,) is essential for progress d industry and the scientific Sharing this knowledge is evolution.

How to eat on the street and (perhaps) live to tell the tale

A real foodie is as conversant in street-food vocabulary as he or she is in the language of haute cuisine. In this age of Tony Bourdain's street chic, you've got to know your *chaat* from your madeleines. This, in theory, is all well and good, until you find yourself in a bustling marketplace in a foreign country, nearly blinded by the colorful array of food on display. Everything looks alluring and ominous in about equal measures. You want to try every delectable mouthful – your foodie street cred depends on it – yet the prospect of spending your vacation in a loving embrace with the comode looms large in your mind. That's not exactly your idea of fun. And you know what? It's not mine either.

Before you assume I have an answer to this dilemma, and then sue me when you come back from your foodie pilgrimage to Oaxaca with a raging case of "Montezuma's revenge," let me tell you I don't have a foolproof procedure that can stop you getting ill from eating bad street food. I don't know anyone who does, not even Tony the Patron Saint of Street Foodies himself. What I can do is offer you a simple guide, one that I follow, and that has so far worked quite well for me. It's just a simple set of rules that will hopefully help you in this situation.

Follow the crowd The locals know what's good and, mostly, what will not make them sick. You're not likely to discover a great food stall that the locals haven't already found out about. Go where the crowd goes, to the most bustling, popular stalls. Even if there's a long line, those people are waiting there for a reason. Be patient. You're on vacation after all.

The popular stalls sell a lot of food. This means that what they are cooking hasn't been sitting around for hours while malevolent germs form a proper colony, waiting to move into your tummy.

Eat hot food (preferably cooked in front of you) The safest bet is to eat only things that are freshly cooked for you, and preferably right in front of you. Food should be "hothot." That means so hot it's uncomfortable to eat, so hot it burns your fingers holding it, and your tongue eating it. We are not talking about just lukewarm. Remember, high heat kills germs. Warm environments just give them a day at the spa, and you don't want to deal with germs that just came from a day at germ spa.

Pack your own utensils Sometimes it's not the food that'll make you sick, it's the improperly cleaned utensils you eat the food with. Moldy, damp bamboo chopsticks washed in murky, barely soaped water is not exactly something I'd use to shuffle food into my mouth. I'm not saying you must pull out your own set of knife and fork at every meal, but packing a few disposable utensils with you on a trip might just come in handy at times. Use your judgment; you will know when you need it. A few disposable chopsticks and a plastic fork or two won't take up that much room in your bag. You will thank me later. Oh, and while you're at it, pack your own tissues too, plenty of them.

Wash your hands often You don't know where everyone else's hands have been, but you can at least keep yours clean. I'm not exactly a believer in hand-sanitizers. Yes, yes, I know they exist. I just don't trust that they work very well. Instead, I always carry a tiny squeeze bottle of soap with me, and wash my hands with it at every opportunity.

Pack some Pepto-Bismol Despite the best precautions, you might get a minor case of the runs. This is more to be expected than something to panic over. Take some over-the-counter remedy along with you, such as Pepto-Bismol, if it makes you more comfortable, but if I were you I wouldn't take anything stronger. Your body is flushing something out for a reason. There's clearly bad stuff in there that should be ousted in a hurry, and the worst thing you could do is put a plug in it.

Think about it for a minute. See what I mean? Just make sure you drink plenty of clean (bottled) water and stay hydrated.

If you peel it you can eat it I have lost track of how many times I got sick from pre-cut fruits I bought from street carts. You don't know where they wash the knife, and worse yet, you don't know where their hands have been. My simple rule about fruits now is, unless I trust the sanitary conditions of the venues, I don't eat any fruit I haven't peeled myself, thank you very much. Bring your own pocket knife – just remember to pack it in your checked luggage before you board the plane.

Take it slow, baby Give your body time to adjust, and don't go all gung-ho the first day you land in a foreign country. Try things you are more certain of at first. Start slowly, and work up to that last-night orgy of street food before you leave for home. At least if you got really sick from it you could be back in time to be treated by your own doctor.

Ten signs of mediocrity

How to spot a mediocre restaurant (and stay away from it)

1. Truffles on the menu in the summer I'm not talking about those luscious, unctuous chocolate truffles. They can be on the menu any day of the year. I am referring to the expensive black Périgord truffle (*Tuber melanosporum*), the black gold from France. Sure, they smell like a stinky old pair of socks to many, but they are also the *ne plus* ultra of *luxe* ingredients.

Pretentious fancy restaurants use black truffles to add a superficial air of refinement to their menu. That is all fine and good until the black truffles go out of season, and the restaurants insist on keeping them on the menu, perhaps because they can't charge as much for a perfect yet simple tomato. Keeping truffles on a year-round menu usually involves the use of those horrid truffle oils, which resemble little and contain even less – if any at all – of the real thing.

Eating seasonally is such a thing these days. Diners are more aware than ever of the quality and seasonality of the produce at their local farmers' market. It's becoming difficult to find sophisticated diners sitting down in the summer heat tucking into a big bowl of earthy beef stew with or without the black truffle-flecked mashed potato (pardon me, *pomme purée*). Truffle on the menu in the summer is a sure sign of a restaurant stuck in another time, and most likely hell-bent on parting you from as much of your money as they can.

2. A million-dollar view or a too convenient location   This rule also covers restaurants that move or rotate atop a frightfully tall building, as well as those that float down a picturesque canal, river, lake, or other famous body of water.

For years, the restaurant Jules Verne on top of the Eiffel Tower was a shining example of how low a restaurant can sink in quality while housed in such a lofty domain. The view was (and is) indeed truly spectacular, but the food was indifferent and the service even more so. And unfortunately it was hardly the exception. Most restaurants with a million-dollar view know what their clientele is there for, and it's usually not the food.

Restaurants with a great location conveniently located, for example, right on a beautiful town square don't need to try very hard to attract customers. Consequently, the food at such places is mediocre at best. This, by the way, doesn't mean that one should never been found dead at one of these establishments. Rather, it's a caution to leave your foodie hat at home or you're sure to be disappointed.

3. The word *gourmet* is used suspiciously often   Like the word *classy*, which is used mostly by those to whom the term does not apply, those who have no idea what *gourmet* means often use the word. Anyone who thinks everything can be made "gourmet" by adding inconsequential and incoherent luxury ingredients, such as dripping truffle oil into an otherwise innocent mashed potato and call it a gourmet mash, should not be taken seriously.

Be particularly wary when "gourmet" is applied to an ethnic cuisine, such as a gourmet Indian restaurant, for example. In such a case it usually just means they've added a tablecloth and perhaps a better brand of soap in the restroom, all of which can result in a massive increase in the prices on the menu, yet only a marginal improvement on the plate, if any.

4. Menu reads like a document from the United Nations   I am not really a fan of fusion, finding it closer to confusion. A case in point is the type of Asian restaurant found in Chinatown in Paris. Some have signs so long they wrap around the building twice, exclaiming "spécialités Chinoise, Thaïlandaise, Vietnamienne, Laötienne, Cambodgienne." They claim to do so many things they can't help but be mediocre at pretty much most of them.

5. Menu is the size of *The Odyssey* It is not entirely practical for a restaurant to stock every conceivable ingredient known to mankind in order to support a menu the length of *The Odyssey*. If they do, the chances are most of the stuff they stock is lolling in the freezer waiting for the day someone finally orders them. I don't know about you, but it's not my idea of fun to order an exotic fish only to find out that it was entombed in the freezer at the same time King Tut was laid to rest in the Valley of the Kings.

An excessively long menu is also a sign that the chef, like a bad writer or artist, doesn't know how to edit himself. No chef can possibly be great at every single recipe in *Larousse Gastronomique*, and listing them all on one menu is just giving the diners a much bigger chance of encountering mediocrity.

6. Unlikely ingredients in unlikely places Someone on an online food board I frequent posted a complaint about a restaurant in Barcelona recently. She had stumbled upon the restaurant, read the menu posted by the front door and, intrigued by the kangaroo meat on offer, went inside. Kangaroo meat. Barcelona. Yes, as in Spain. The meal was less than satisfactory. She expressed a mild outrage at the outcome. I would have said it was to be expected. One might even say she asked for it.

A travel writer complained in the pages of an august paper recently of a mediocre dish he ate at a restaurant high up in the northern region of Thailand. He was somehow led to believe that a dish of stir-fried stone crab was the speciality of the house, and dutifully ordered it up for the table. The town in which the restaurant is located is far up toward the northernmost border of Thailand, hours away from the nearest body of seawater. Of course the dish was mediocre. In fact I was surprised it hadn't been a downright horror. The writer would have had far better luck ordering local freshwater fish from the abundant rivers nearby.

This is not to say that it is not possible to ship crabs to the north of Thailand, or that only restaurants in Australia can serve kangaroo meat and do it well. However, unless there's an extraordinary circumstance (the owner was an Australian who moved to Spain and whose father operated a kangaroo farm), chances are the restaurant offers kangaroo more as a curiosity than anything delicious to eat.

7. Ushers at the door Good restaurants don't need to have people standing by the front door waving hello to tourists and beckoning them to come in. It's usually the other way round. Fabulous restaurants go to great lengths to find gatekeepers to prevent people from entering, albeit in the most tactful way possible.

8. "Twenty locations in ten cities all over the world!" Hard Rock Café. Need I say more?

9. Restaurant has a gift shop attached This is particularly worrying if such a gift shop carries a fluffy toy or teddy bear bearing the name or insignia of the restaurant. There's an exception to this rule, however. Many three-star restaurants in the French countryside feature a shop selling local products or special ingredients created by the chef, and these can be wonderful. I've had great success cooking with spices I bought from the shop next to La Maison de Bricourt in Cancale. The chef, Olivier Roellinger, is famous for his deft use of exotic spices, and the speciality blends he sells at the stores are just fabulous. I've also brought back many a delicious bite from the gift shop at Michel Bras's restaurant. Still, most restaurants with gift shops attached are, well… Hard Rock Café, anyone?

10. Restaurant is empty As a general rule, an empty restaurant is quite likely a mediocre one as well. Don't assume that you'll find an undiscovered gem hiding in the dirt while traveling in some exotic locale. If the restaurant were any good, someone else, most likely the locals, would have found out before you.

Sushi bar 101

One of my favorite guides to eating sushi is a video I found on
YouTube. It's a spoof, mind you, complete with farcical moments
recounting how to seat yourself and your friends, precisely where to
place your hands on the (hinoho wood) sushi bar as you – reverentially –
give your order to the chef. It goes on to explain which three fingers
to use, and how precisely to deploy them on a piece of sushi, how to
properly dip a *nigiri*, and at which angle to tilt your head as you place it
– gingerly, of course – into your mouth. It also covers how to order from
a secret menu (of *course* there's a secret menu!). In the long tradition of
great satires, the outrageous hyperboles in the video betray more than a
few grains of truth. It's truth-y, as Stephen Colbert would say.

    Going to a sushi bar is such a mythical, foreign experience
fraught with peril – or at least potential embarrassments – that it easily
sets people off in vain in search of a foolproof ten-step how-to. The
Internet is riddled with them, and a quick Google search confirms as
much. Let me just tell you, if you're hoping to find that how-to here,
you are mistaken. It simply does not exist.

    At eight out of ten sushi bars, the chef, the waiters, and the
proprietor are not going to care one little bit how you behave. What
they want is for you to eat up, drink up, pay up, and get up so that the
next customer can sit down and take his turn at eating up, drinking up,
paying up, and getting up, so that the next, next customer can take his

turn. You get the point. It's easy enough to spot this quick-turnover type of sushi bar. They are usually a large and, if they are lucky, bustling establishment. They often have an extensive non-sushi menu, and certainly with a few "bento boxes" to choose from with combinations largely dominated by teriyaki chicken or tempura, which invariably come garnished with an artfully twisted slice of orange.

Any attempt by foreigners to follow some elaborate – half imagined – rituals will only be met with bemusement on the part of the staff. They wouldn't say so, of course, but that's what the chatter in Japanese between the chef and the waiters is about. That you place the fish top-down or bottom-up as it passes your lips into the concave of your mouth isn't going to make your cash go further than the next person's. Ignore exotic anecdotes about not rubbing your chopsticks together because it would be considered rude: it is worse form for a restaurant to serve chopsticks with splinters to you. So just stop worrying and eat, though, of course, normal etiquette applies.

What do you do at these places then, you ask? Besides trying not to find yourself in one, my advice is simple: eat what everyone else is eating. Mediocre to mid-range sushi bars operate by the law of turnovers. The better the turnover, the better the sushi. The more common the sushi, the more often people ask for them, the fresher they will be, and the less likely for you to pick up something a course or two of antibiotics wouldn't fix. Here you would be ill advised to order aoyaki clam or abalone with a sauce made of its liver just to show off your knowledge of obscure sushi. Chances are those Aoyaki clams have been lolling, fermenting, waiting to strike the collective vengeance of the entire species upon just such an overachieving poseur. "Keep it simple" is the key to survival here. I would also stay away from rolls made of chopped fish often served swimming in cloying sauce: the perfect way to mask old fish and pawn it off as "speciality of the house." Come to think of it, eat the damned well-done chicken teriyaki and be done with it.

Your goal in your (sushi-eating) life, instead, should be finding the other two out of ten sushi bars, the ones that are actually worth the effort to visit. They don't have to be fancy. They don't even have to be big. They just have to be run by people who care, and frequented by other diners who care just as much. Spotting these genuine sushi bars is so easy, you can almost tell them apart from a first glance in the room.

You won't ever find great sushi at a messy restaurant. Great sushi is a fastidious business, so the bar should be spotlessly clean and always especially tidy.

What's on offer at these places is often simple, with fresh fish for the day displayed in a refrigerated glass case. You won't find speciality rolls made with tempura prawns, wrapped in rice and over it a layer of avocado, encased in seaweed, soaked in sticky sweet sauce, and served – just to damn yourself properly – with a side of soy sauce and a big dab of green goo pretending to be wasabi. Instead, you will find pristine fish and other seafood served on top of well seasoned rice. There may indeed be a few cooked dishes, but that part of the menu shouldn't be so extensive as to obscure the real star of the show, the sushi.

When you find yourself a sushi-ya like this, don't bother reading anything up about it on the Internet or in magazines, not even in a book. Just go there as frequently as you can. Your goal is to ingratiate yourself into the good graces of the house. The rule of politeness here is not any different than anywhere else. Eat what looks interesting to you but try new things occasionally, too. Ask questions that show that you care. Wait your turn to order, and remember that a sushi meal is never fast food. Wrap your head around that concept and you will be just fine.

Then there is the one out of every hundred sushi bars, or perhaps even one in a thousand, which is so rare a breed I left it completely off the first equation. Going to a sushi bar like this is more akin to entering a battlefield or perhaps starting a kung fu lesson with a cranky old master, a *sifu* in a conspicuously girly gown (think *Kill Bill*). You must prove yourself worthy before you are let in on the secret and taught the Five-Point-Palm-Exploding-Heart-Technique, or be simply served a proper meal of sushi. Otherwise you'll just get the round-eye specials and ushered quickly through a meal, from which you emerge with a hole the size of a month's worth of rent in your wallet.

One must not enter such exalted a realm without proper introduction. In fact, one is likely never to be allowed entrance to begin with. One such famous sushi bar in the ultra-expensive Ginza district of Tokyo is known to hang up the phone when English is spoken, or even insufficiently polite Japanese.

The only way to go is *omakase*, trusting the sushi master to choose for you. Learn the speciality of the house, not to order, but to *ooh* and *ahh* appropriately when one is served to you. It is up to you to prove your worth to the master behind the bar. Remember that you are being watched at every moment. Even dipping a piece of sushi in the soy sauce is considered an affront. Yes, the house provides the soy sauce, but it is a generous offer that you must not take up. It's almost impossible to list every possible scenario in which you might make a fool of yourself in a place like this, so I suppose the most sensible advice is for you to find a good friend – preferably a local, and someone known to the house – to take you. Watch them closely, follow their every move, and pray they actually know what they're doing.

Just like a grueling training with a kung fu master, the resulting epiphany resulting from a meal like this can be transcendent, and will be costly. Just ask Uma Thurman.

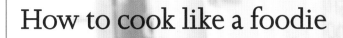

2 | How to cook like a foodie

Buy the best ingredients you can afford

As much as we love to eat, dining out every single day sounds more like a punishment. Foodie or not, when faced with throwing a few ingredients in a pot to make dinner for ourselves, we can all do it. And unless you're one of those lucky souls who are either rich enough to afford a full-time private chef or lucky enough to have a partner who does it all for you, we all cook to feed ourselves. Some of us foodies even find it fun.

Cooking needn't be a chore, and shouldn't be boring. It is high time we learned to cook and think like a foodie, spice up our cooking life and kick it up the proverbial notch. Why *not* get a Michelin star for your home kitchen?

The first step to being a foodie, as any chef will tell you, is to buy the best ingredient you can afford, because great food begins with good ingredients. Food made with bad ingredients is often masked by fat, sugar, and salt to create a façade of taste so it becomes palatable. If you don't believe me, go and buy a Big Mac and taste it. A bite from the whole burger isn't so bad: savory meat, a sweetish sauce, a little crunch from the lettuce. Then try each component separately. You'll taste the insipid meat; the spongy, soggy bread; and the wilted, watery lettuce, all of which become edible only with the help of fatty processed cheese and salty and sugary sauces. In contrast, think back to the last time you had a really great piece of steak or a simple roast chicken. They were probably flavored by not much more than salt and pepper.

Buy a good free-range chicken that had a happy life, and taste it side-by-side with a cheap generic supermarket chicken. You can immediately tell the difference in the flavor and texture. Buy good meat that comes from animals raised and slaughtered humanely instead of those that have been intensely fed on grain and raised in confined quarters. If not to mitigate the environmental effects of those practices, then do it for the taste, because cows in the latter case generally grow too fast to have developed a good flavor or proper muscle texture. Buy fresh vegetables because it means you won't need to cook them with so much butter and sugar to make them tasty. Mind you, there's nothing wrong with adding butter, but you should do it because you prefer to and not because you must.

I don't want to get into the un-winnable argument about organic food being overpriced and out of the reach of "real" people with "real" budgets. I completely empathize with budget concerns. (I was once a starving graduate student myself.) I also agree that an inexpensive supermarket chicken cooked with fresh vegetables and tender loving care at home will taste infinitely better than any frozen TV dinner you can buy. If the choice is between buying a conventional chicken or having no protein at all then, by all means, forget organic. I would, however, like to point out that comparing the cost of organic or conventional chickens is not as simple as putting two numbers next to each other. Often overlooked in the monetary value of conventional chickens and other foods are the hidden costs we bear in the form of subsidized corn production, pesticide manufacturing, and other environmental costs. Pick up a copy of Michael Pollan's masterpiece *The Omnivore's Dilemma* for all the arguments you'll ever need to hear on this important matter. Meanwhile, as for us, let's get off the soapbox and back into the kitchen, shall we?

When speaking of great ingredients, one thing we often overlook is the pantry. It doesn't matter how much you pay for that pristine designer lettuce fresh from Borough Market. Dress it in inferior olive oil and all you get is a B-list celebrity pretending to be pretty in her questionable outfits.

Check in your pantry and see what kind of ingredients live there. How old is your olive oil? Your mustard? That vinegar? You'd be surprised how many people just buy and then cook with ingredients without having really tasted each individually to see what they are like at all. For example, does your olive oil just taste greasy and smell vaguely of little else except dirt? If it's been in your pantry a while it might be time to replace it. How old is the garlic, or the onions or shallots? Are they so old they have green shoots breaking out of the top? Take a clove of garlic, and smash it with the flat side of a knife blade. Do you hear an indignant crunch or does it just make a whimper? Throw out that whimpering old garlic – it'll just give you heartburn later.

Having a supply of good pasta, canned tomatoes, and perhaps basil-scented olive oil on hand means you can whip up a quick pasta dinner any day of the week. The same goes for anchovies or plump capers. And being Asian, I always have at least three kinds of rice in my pantry.

It would be difficult to put together a list of essential pantry ingredients, because we all cook so differently. Trust me, there are plenty of things I consider must-haves on my kitchen shelves that you wouldn't know how to spell, let alone know what to do with. The better solution is to look at how you yourself love to cook, make a list of ingredients that you use often, and make sure that you buy them in the highest quality you can afford. So you see, we can all be foodies in our own way.

Be a market groupie

Embrace your inner teenage groupie. Foodie groupies don't put on their best Oasis T-shirt and faint at the mere sight of Liam on stage, but they might at a glimpse of Randolph behind the counter at Neal's Yard Dairy at Borough Market in London. Okay, perhaps not Randolph. How about Joe at the Dirty Girl farm stall at the Saturday farmers' market in San Francisco? Seriously. Have you seen Joe?

Joking aside, the best way to learn about great ingredients and get them into your kitchen is to make friends with the people who sell them. This could be at your local supermarket, gourmet deli, farmers' markets, or even directly from food producers themselves. Find people whose food you like and support them with your patronage. Ask them questions, give them feedback, and just talk to them. People who are passionate about food are always eager to share what they know.

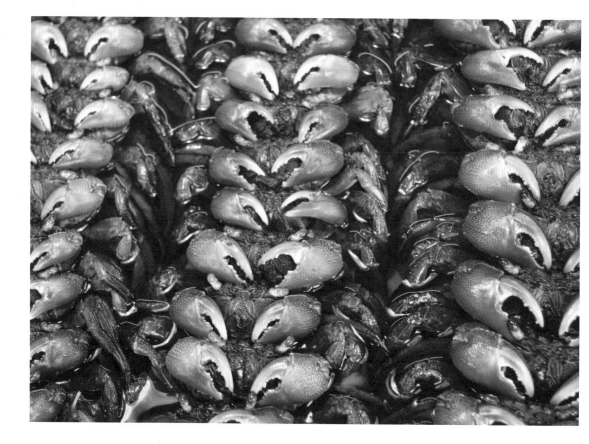

Trust me on this. Haven't you seen how many food blogs there are out there? We foodies are an expressive bunch.

I am a firm believer in supporting the people who supply great food to our table. In return, I've learned a lot of valuable lessons from them. When I first moved to San Francisco nearly ten years ago, there was a tiny cheese shop just a few blocks down the hill from my flat in Pacific Heights. The shop was so small I wondered how the business could last, and it sure didn't. One day I walked by to find it was shuttered up for good. I was crushed. Sure, the shopkeeper was a grumpy French guy, and the shop often smelled of stinky old socks, but his cheeses had been better than anything I could get at the local markets. Luckily, a few weeks later a new cheese mini-empire opened, and instead of the grumpy French guy there was a cheery woman in his place. Her name was Peggy. I became a regular customer.

The specter of awful, sweaty, shrink-wrapped cheese at the supermarket still haunting me, I was determined to do my darndest to help keep that little cheese shop in business. Living alone, I didn't buy a

lot of cheese, but I made a point of buying as often as I could. Peggy was delightful. Her passion for the products she sold was palpable and infectious. She always gave me a taste of this cheese and that, giving me a valuable lesson with every purchase. With her help, I evolved quite rapidly from thinking that Cheddar was that dubious orange cheese you peel from its plastic casing and put in a burger to knowing the finer points of Keen's versus Montgomery Cheddars. It's the kind of knowledge you aren't gonna learn reading a book – even one as great as the book in your hands right now. I started calling her my cheese godmother. As it turned out, my fairy-cheesy godmother Peggy is not just any Peggy, but Peggy Smith, one of the two founders of what is now a mini-cheese empire, Cowgirl Creamery, in San Francisco. She once worked for Alice Waters at Chez Panisse, which in the Bay Area culinary term is akin to being of royal blood. Peggy has over the years been my entrée to many a foodie circle in San Francisco and beyond. I am a better foodie for it, and of course forever grateful. Find your own Peggy and you will be, too.

Learn how to cook, not to follow recipes

Painting by numbers will never get you a Rembrandt, just as cooking by recipes will never give you a Michelin star. Legendary French chef Alain Chapel once compared recipes to prison. No, not the kind where people wear striped uniforms. He probably only meant a prison that limits your imagination, your creativity and all that jazz. My friend Daniel Patterson, the articulate chef of Coi in San Francisco, explained to me that following a recipe rigidly is like driving with your GPS switched on. It tells you when to turn left, or right, add a cupful of this and a teaspoonful of that, but at the end of the day, when the GPS fails, you won't know how to find your way back home or put a soup on the table.

Recipes are often written in such a clinical fashion. I especially detest the overly precise ones that tell you to cook *this* for exactly five minutes and then add *precisely* three tablespoon of *that*. How would they know that five minutes over "moderate" heat on my stove would be the same as on theirs? As a recovering scientist I struggle with the whole slew of potential determining variables, the thickness of the pan, the intensity of heat on the stove, the temperature of the food itself, just to name a few. Five minutes on my stove may not be five minutes on someone else's. In addition, precise measurement of seasonings doesn't take into account individual taste and preferences. I prefer recipes that are written expressively, explaining what would happen and why, teaching us to taste and to be on the lookout for how the food develops along the way.

My friend, jazz impresario Wynton Marsalis, once explained to me his main criteria for inviting musicians into his famous company, Jazz at Lincoln Center. He looks for musicians with a large vocabulary. No, he's not talking about the kind in the OED, but vocabulary of music: the tunes, the tempos, and knowledge of the way Thelonious Monk, Louis Armstrong, or Duke Ellington played. Great musicians, Wynton asserted, were the ones who understood the vocabulary of all the great musicians before them so they could react to and improvise with the band. Cooking is so much like jazz, the success of a particular dish or a tune depends largely on how well the improvisation works. Just as jazz musicians don't follow sheet music note by note, cooks shouldn't, or couldn't, follow a recipe to the letter.

HOW TO COOK LIKE A FOODIE

I'm not arguing that recipes are completely useless. Even great jazz musicians don't compose a whole new tune every time they play. Good recipes give you a guideline, a roadmap to follow, teach you what to expect and show you how to build certain flavors and textures in a particular dish. It is then up to you to improvise with the circumstances you find yourself in on a given day. When the bass player in your band sets a tune to a certain tempo, it's up to you to know where he's going with it and improvise your response. Things are not that different with a leg of lamb in your oven.

The best way to build your cooking vocabulary is to cook. Try your hand at some basic recipes. Learn how to roast a chicken, cook a fish, or make pastry dough. Think of each recipe as teaching you a particular technique. Learn how to tell when a chicken is done by how it looks or smells. Learn how to tell the doneness of a piece of steak by touching it: no one can really tell you what it feels like. You must build your own muscle memory from trying it yourself.

The first lesson: how to roast a chicken

Before you learn to sail, first you learn how to row a little boat. No book can adequately describe the sensation of being a part of the current, the wind, and the ocean the way rowing a little boat can show you. To sail you must first understand how to feel those elements, and so you row a little boat.

Learning to cook is much the same. No recipe can describe exactly how to make a dish in fine enough details that you will never fail using it. Only experience can teach you how to feel the food as it is cooking, so first you learn with something simple. A chicken, roasted with not much more than a bit of salt and pepper as seasoning, will teach you a great deal. You will taste your success, and when you make a mistake, you'll know it, too. You will learn how to be flexible with a recipe, as no two chickens are exactly alike, nor do all ovens behave the same way. Following a recipe blindly just will not do. You must learn how to use your eyes, ears, and nose, and to make adjustments as you go along. Before you know it, you'll be able to tell when a chicken is done by the way it smells, or even how it moves when you give a leg a little jiggle.

On the roasting of chicken

Every foodie worth his or her salt must know how to roast a good chicken. No, I'm not talking about just simply knowing how to cook a chicken. I meant roasting it *properly*, to the crisp skin and golden glory of it all. Great chefs each have their own method of doing it. Thomas Keller has no fewer than three published recipes for roast chicken, one of which involves scrubbing the skin of the chicken thoroughly with mounds of expensive fleur de sel. Alain Passard, at his three-star L'Arpège in Paris, roasts his chicken not in the oven at all but on the stove top, affectionately turning and basting the bird constantly with good salted butter from his native Brittany. Alain's roast chicken is glorious but, unlike him, I don't have the patience – or a line cook – to stand by the roasting pan doing all the turning and basting until the chicken is golden brown all over.

My roast chicken salvation arrived when I discovered The One True Method That Rules Them All. I'm referring to what is known as *la méthode Robuchon*, as taught to me (well, not personally) by Patricia Wells in her book *Simply French*. That's the only way I do a roast chicken. No. That's the only way to do a roast chicken.

The genius of *la méthode Robuchon* is not about the seasoning or the accompaniment – look to Alain Ducasse for all that fancy stuffing and sauces. Robuchon's thing is all about the technique. First roast the chicken on its side, resting on a thigh, then flip over to rest on the other, and finish with the breast up. This way, the thighs are cooked first, with the skin in full contact with the heat so they are nicely crisp. The breast is cooked last, preserving the yummy juiciness inside. In the end, the bird is put to rest before carving in a certain position, breast down and tail up, forcing all the juice to flow down and keep the breast deliciously moist.

That's all there is to it. No matter how you season it, or the size of the chicken, or what you cook alongside it to give it flavor, this method works beautifully, always. Trust me. You'll try this once and be hooked, too. Bravo Robuchon! (*And brava Mme Wells!*)

Over the years I've added my own touches, using tidbits borrowed (and/or stolen) from other noted chefs and great cooks. The most important change I made to *la méthode* is what goes inside the chicken. M. Robuchon advises no more than salt and pepper, but I always stuff my chicken. Not a fancy stuffing intended to be served at table *à la Ducasse*, mind you. I use just an onion and perhaps a few herbs or aromatics to add flavor and to keep the breast from drying out. This is a trick I learned from Harold McGee. A hollow chicken cooks not just from the outside but also from the inside out, especially in the breast area, Harold explained. Stuffing the cavity of the chicken prevents hot air from circulating too freely in there, drying out the breast, which is the most exposed even on the inside. Makes sense, yes, as he often does.

Another thing worth noting before you embark on this chicken-roasting journey is the quality of the raw ingredient. Monsieur Robuchon simply assumes – being French and all – that the chicken intended for the roast is of good quality. I doubt he's ever tried a British supermarket chicken. Mushy, pale, and waterlogged, they are fit for hardly anything but the KFC fryer. That's not something you want to labor over. To cook a perfect roast chicken one must begin with a perfect chicken, or at least one that has aspirations toward perfection. I suggest you buy a (previously) happy chicken that has spent part of its life outside, tromping on Gods' good earth. Chickens that have been fed a proper diet, free from antibiotics and growth hormones and countless other things you'd rather not put in your body, because, you know, that's precisely where that chicken is heading.

You won't even need any fancy, special equipment. Don't bother with the roasting rack or even an expensive roasting pan. I use a rectangular flameproof Pyrex baking dish that's not that much bigger than the chicken itself. One special piece of equipment I do recommend you buy is a baster, one of those tubular gadgets that slurp up the pan juice so you can drop it back over the chicken to keep it nice and moist. You don't need it to roast a perfect chicken, but it does save you from having to awkwardly spoon up sizzling hot pan juice to baste the chicken while it is cooking.

Okay. Now that's squared away, we can begin our roast.

Ingredients for a perfect roast chicken

3¹/₄ lb | 1.5kg good-quality chicken
3 tablespoons soft butter
1 to 2 tablespoons good salt and a good dose of freshly ground black pepper
1 medium-sized onion
1 to 2 heads garlic, to taste
a few sprigs of fresh thyme and rosemary

You start by preheating the oven to 425°F/220°C/Gas Mark 7. Give your chicken a quick rinse and pat it thoroughly dry with paper towels. Rub the chicken generously with soft butter. (If all you have is the cold butter fresh from the fridge, just give it a quick whirl in the microwave to soften it.) Massage that baby nice and good. As Julia Child would say, "Give it some love." If you have the patience (and the dexterity) gently insert your hand under the chicken skin to separate it from the body. This step is not for everyone. You must do this carefully and try not to break the skin, so skip it if you're not up to it. Your chicken will still be just fine. Now, sprinkle the bird inside and out liberally with salt, a lot of it. Rub it all in with conviction. When in doubt, throw in a little more. Crack some pepper and give the bird a good shower with it, too.

Monsieur Robuchon suggests trussing the bird. Of course he does, being a fancy chef and all. I do it from time to time, but if you're intimidated by the mere thought of putting your bird in bondage, you don't have to. Tying the bird will make it easier to turn it though. If you don't know how to truss a chicken, just take two pieces of kitchen twine, use one to pull the end of the two legs together and tie them tight, and the other to strap the wings tightly to the breast. You can do it. Use your imagination! (If you really want to learn how to properly truss a chicken, go Google it or buy Jacques Pépin's book *Complete Techniques*.)

Then you stuff that baby. My usual quick stuffing is just an onion cut into quarters. If I have some leeks around I might use the green top, which is not much use for anything else except soup. Sometimes I even use lemon halves. Whatever you have on hand that can lend some good flavors, just use them. I always add a few fresh herbs to the stuffing as well, perhaps a few sprigs of rosemary, thyme, or even tarragon, depending on what I have to hand. A clove of garlic or two (or twenty) will do as well.

Take a roasting pan and rub a tiny bit of butter on the bottom just to be safe. Put the chicken down on its side, resting on one of the thighs. If the chicken comes with the neck, throw it in alongside. Take one or two bulbs of garlic, cut them horizontally in half and add them to the pan (cut-side up), adding another sprig or two of thyme and rosemary.

The chicken goes into the middle of the oven lopsided, just like that. Hang out for about 30 minutes, after which you pull out the tin, baste it, and give the chicken a little flip so that it rests on the other thigh. Roast for another 30 minutes. Then flip again once more so the breast side is up. Baste it, and continue cooking for 20 more minutes. I do all these flipping actions with the aid of two big wooden spoons, because they won't cut through the skin the way metal tongs do.

After the 20 minutes (with the breast upward) is over, check to see if the chicken is done. You can tell by poking a metal skewer or the tip of a knife into the thick part of the thigh. If the juice runs clear, then your chicken is done. If not, turn the heat down to 375°F/190°C/Gas Mark 5 and continue to cook until the juice runs clear, which usually takes no more than 10 to 20 minutes, depending on the size of your chicken. Remove it from the oven as soon as it is done and turn the heat off.

Lift the chicken out of the roasting pan and put it on a large platter. This also requires a bit of dexterity. Place your chicken with its neck down, tail in the air. It's rather immodest but the chicken is beyond caring. I find one or two strategically placed upturned coffee cups work well to hold the chicken in place. This way, the juice will run down to the breast as the chicken rests.

Cover the plate loosely with aluminum foil to keep the chicken warm. Let it rest either on your work surface or inside the oven (make sure it's turned off) with the door ajar. The chicken must rest for at least 10 minutes before you can carve it.

Meanwhile, you can make a quick *jus*, or pan sauce. (Would it be less intimidating if I called it gravy?) Whatever you call it, it's super-easy and your chicken will be grateful for it.

FOR THE JUS
salt and pepper, to taste
1/2 cup | 110ml red wine or water (or a couple splashes of Vermouth)
1 teaspoon red wine or sherry vinegar
pat of butter

Begin by removing the garlic halves and setting them aside to serve with the chicken. Set the roasting pan directly on the stove over medium heat. Deglaze it with some sort of liquid. I often use about half a glass of red wine (if you're drinking some) or sometimes a splash or two of vermouth. Water will also do in a pinch. In fact, I usually add a little water anyway if I'm using vermouth. Then, the final trick, learned from my partner David Kinch, is a teaspoon of red wine or sherry vinegar. It brightens the flavor and rounds out the saltiness of the sauce. Scrape up all the delicious bits that cling to the pan. Skim off the excess fat. When you've finished scraping, turn the heat to low and let it simmer for a bit until thickened. A few minutes usually suffice.

When the sauce is ready, strain it into a sauce boat to serve. If you want to be really decadent, drop a pat (you choose the size) of butter into the sauce, and shake the pan to dissolve it into the sauce before straining.

Serve the chicken with a side dish of your choice.

Easy Roast Potatoes

I don't like to roast potatoes right next to the chicken in the roasting pan, because they interfere with the beautiful pan juice I need for the jus later. You could still have lovely "roast" potatoes – crisp at the edges and infused with the roast chicken's essence – by following this simple recipe. Do this while the chicken is in the oven and you can finish the potatoes while the chicken is resting just before serving.

You will need about 2lb/1kg of potatoes for four servings. I use new potatoes no bigger than 2in/5cm in diameter. Take a frying pan large enough to fit all the potatoes in one layer, add the potatoes to it and enough water to just cover them. Add a few pinches of salt and about 2 tablespoons of butter. Set the pan on the stove over high heat until the water is boiling. Reduce the heat to medium and let it simmer until the potatoes are completely cooked through. This should take about 20 to 30 minutes, depending on the size of the potatoes. Drain the liquid and leave the cooked potatoes in the pan.

When the chicken is done and resting, skim some fat from the roasting pan and set the pan aside. Using the bottom of a glass or cup, gently crush each potato until it is lightly smashed. Pour the chicken fat you've just skimmed from the pan all over the potatoes, adding a tablespoon or two more butter if you want. Turn the heat back up to high and cook the potatoes until they are brown and crispy on both sides. Sprinkle over a bit of salt and a few turns of the peppermill, and serve with the roast chicken.

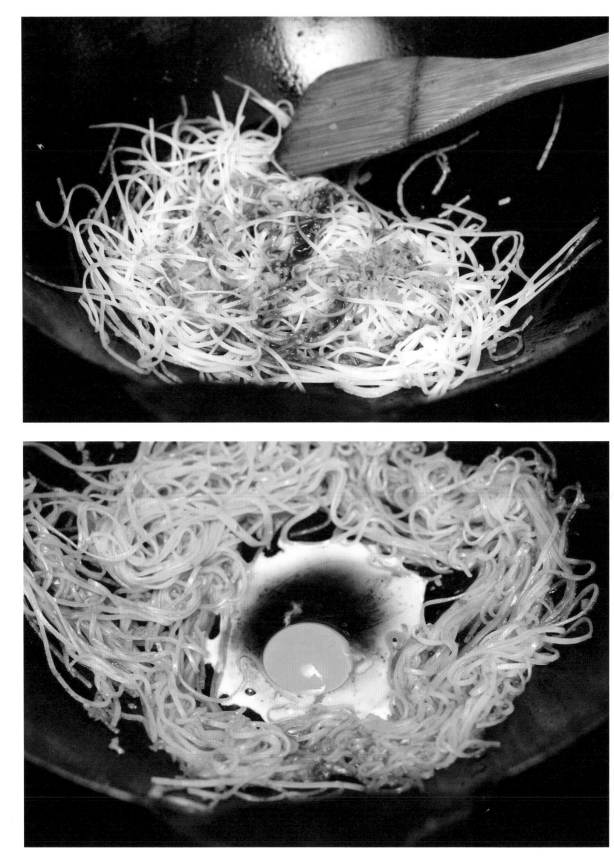

Pad Thai for beginners

The most popular recipe I've ever posted on my blog Chez Pim is my Pad Thai recipe. I called it Pad Thai for Beginners, and it's been linked a thousand times over on the very popular shared bookmarks site del.icio.us and other Internet sites. It has generated hundreds of e-mails and comments from readers who have tried it and loved the results. Calling it a Pad Thai recipe is a misnomer, however. In fact, it's an anti-recipe, and a perfect example of what cooking is all about. It proves what I've been saying here because the key to making a great Pad Thai rests on a good understanding of the process and not on a precise recipe. Unlike Western ingredients, Asian ingredients are not standardized. For example, different brands of fish sauce are not equally salty; some palm sugars are sweeter than others. Specifying precise amounts of those ingredients is therefore even more difficult.

To make a great Pad Thai, you must understand four things: the wok, the sauce, the ingredients, and the cooking process.

The wok
(I'm going to assume that you have a wok that is well seasoned. If not, get one, or use a Western-style frying pan at least 11- to 12-in (28- to 30-cm) wide. If you have a brand-new wok, you'll need to season it first*, see next page.)

The difference between properly done, deliciously charred Pad Thai and a gooey glob of sticky noodles swimming in cloying sauce is the heat of the wok. Most woks are made of thin carbon steel, and with use, the wok's inside surface develops a patina, which lends a delicious "wok-breath" or char to any dish cooked in it. Carbon steel is a great conduit of heat, but doesn't retain it well. This is a very important point, because for the food to cook properly you can only do one or two portions at a time. That is precisely how the Pad Thai vendors in Bangkok do it.

In order to give each plate of your Pad Thai the char it needs, you have to start cooking when the pan is smoking hot, and keep the pan that way the whole way through. This means your ingredients must be as close to room temperature as possible, so they won't bring down the temperature in the wok as you add them.

* HOW TO SEASON A WOK: There are a number of ways to season a wok. Here's how I do it. First, pour 1 cup/255ml of oil into the wok. Tilt the wok all around to coat the entire inside surface with the oil. Place the wok over high heat and leave it until it is smoking. Tilt the pan to keep the sides coated and let it continue to smoke for a few minutes. Remove the wok from the heat and carefully dispose of the hot oil. Pour half a cup of kosher or large-grain salt into the wok. Using a clean rag, rub the salt all over the inside of the wok. Discard the salt, and wipe the wok clean with a damp towel. You may rinse it if you want. Pour a small amount of oil onto a paper towel and wipe it all over the inside surface again. Your wok is now seasoned and ready.

The sauce

Here's another thing we could learn from street vendors in Bangkok: they make their Pad Thai sauce beforehand. It not only streamlines the cooking in the wok, but also ensures that you can calibrate the flavor of the sauce to your liking. Imagine trying to do that while juggling not overcooking the prawns or the noodles in the wok.

There are four ingredients in Pad Thai sauce, which balance out the traditional flavor components in Thai cooking: tamarind pulp (sour), fish sauce (salty), palm sugar (sweet), and Thai chili powder or paprika (hot). Two cups of the sauce will make about six to eight portions of Pad Thai. You can make as little or as much as you need, because the sauce will keep well in the fridge for weeks. I usually make enough to keep on hand to soothe any emergency Pad Thai cravings.

To make about 2 cups/400 ml of sauce, you should begin with about 1/2 cup/100ml each of tamarind** (see the note on facing page for how to prepare tamarind pulp), fish sauce, and palm sugar. If you substitute white and/or brown sugar for the palm sugar, you should use only about 1/3 cup/80g. Melt all these together in a small saucepan over low heat. Taste and adjust the flavor until it suits you. Then add the chili powder, beginning with a teaspoon or two, depending on your taste, and keep adding until it tastes the way you like it. By the time you're done adjusting the flavoring the pot should be simmering happily. Turn off the heat and let the sauce rest while you get to the other ingredients.

At this point, I like my sauce to lead with a salty flavor, followed by a mild sourness, then just a gentle sweetness and a soft caress from the chili at the back of my throat at the very end. A finished plate of Pad Thai will be served with a sliver of lime and extra chili powder to be mixed in at the table, so you can keep these two flavors mild in the sauce for now. Be careful not to make the sauce too sweet right now because it will be very tough to correct later.

A NOTE ON TAMARIND: You can buy tamarind in blocks or ready-made pulp in plastic or glass containers. If you can't find a local market that carries tamarind you can order it online. If you buy ready-made pulp, check to make sure it contains only tamarind and water, and no sugar or anything else. If you buy tamarind in a block, soak it in 4 cups/1 litre of hot water in a large bowl and let it sit until the water has cooled down enough not to scald your hands. Stick your hands ("your impeccably clean hands," as Julia Child would say) into the bowl and work the tamarind and water together until the consistency is a bit looser than room-temperature ketchup. Add more warm water if needed. Then, strain the mixture to remove the seeds and tough membranes from the tamarind pulp. The consistency will be thick, so you'll need to press it through the sieve. Use as much as you need for the Pad Thai sauce and keep the rest sealed in a glass jar in your fridge. You'll have tamarind pulp handy for a long time. This recipe is highly adaptable. If you don't like the intensity of tamarind, you can substitute up to half the amount with rice vinegar.

Pad Thai ingredients

These are the ingredients that compose the Pad Thai noodle dish. It's difficult to specify the quantity of each one, as how much or little you use of them is entirely up to you.

THIN RICE NOODLES, ALSO CALLED RICE STICKS: Here you should try to find Thai rice sticks, and they should not be confused with the Vietnamese variety. The Thai rice noodles used in Pad Thai look something like fettuccine, only whiter, and perhaps just a bit thinner, while the Vietnamese ones are shaped like spaghetti. Thai rice sticks are sometimes labeled Pad Thai noodles or *sen lek* noodles.

Get them fresh if you can find them at an Asian supermarket. If not, buy dried noodles and soak them in slightly warm water (the noodles should be soft, but not quite softened through that you could actually eat it without cooking, or they will turn into mush in the wok. Soak them until they are just pliable, and then make sure you drain them well. You will need a good handful per portion, but you can use more or less as you like. It is entirely up to you and your friends. A 1lb/500g pack of dried noodles should be enough for six to eight portions, but buy a little extra just to be sure. They are cheap and, if left unsoaked, will last just about forever.

Depending on the freshness of your "fresh" rice noodles, you might want to soak them anyway just to soften them a bit more. Follow the same step as for the dried noodles but do not soak them as long. One 1lb/500g bag of fresh noodles will be enough for three to four portions.

PRAWNS OR CHICKEN: *(For vegetarians see Tofu below.)*
Traditional Pad Thai uses prawns. I usually use about seven medium-sized peeled prawns per portion. When I find perfectly fresh large prawns with head and roe intact, I don't bother peeling them at all. I slice them right through the middle and use them whole.

You can also easily substitute chicken for the prawns. Serve about 2oz/50g of chicken meat, cut into bite-sized pieces, per portion. This will be plenty.

TOFU: I like to use the pressed tofu that comes in square blocks. You can use just about any firm-textured tofu you can find, even the pre-fried varieties you can buy in Chinese supermarkets. As long as it doesn't disintegrate when fried in the wok, it will be suitable. I cut the tofu into thin, bite-sized pieces and use about a small handful in each carnivorous portion. For a vegetarian portion with no meat, you will have to use more. Also, to make it completely vegetarian, you can use thin soy sauce in place of the fish sauce.

EGGS: I usually crack one small egg into the wok while cooking each serving. If you like less egg in your Pad Thai you can make two servings at a time and only crack in one egg, essentially cutting the egg quantity in half in each portion.

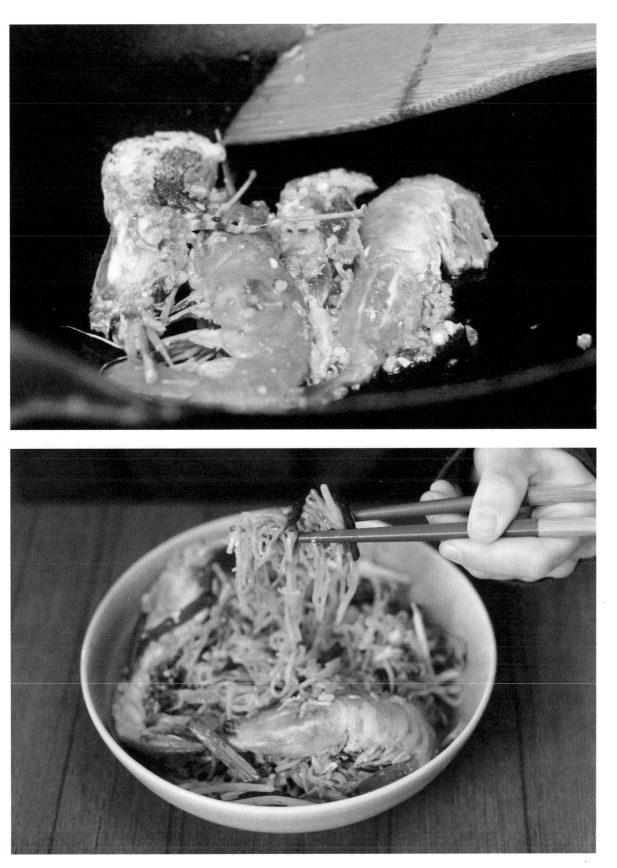

GROUND PEANUTS: I use roasted and unsalted peanuts (sometimes I roast my own) for this. Grind the peanuts roughly, but be careful not to overdo it. Otherwise you will end up with peanut butter and not ground peanuts. You will need 1 to 2 tablespoons per portion, depending on how much your friends like peanuts.

FLAT-LEAF GARLIC CHIVES, ALSO CALLED CHINESE CHIVES: Although most restaurants use the green part of spring onions, garlic chives are the more traditional herb for Pad Thai. Wash and dry the chives well, then cut them into 2-inch (5-cm) pieces. I use a handful per portion.

BEAN SPROUTS: I love a lot of bean sprouts in my Pad Thai, so I use a good handful per portion. You can use as much or little as you like. My sister opts to skip them entirely.

PICKLED TURNIPS (OPTIONAL): You can buy pickled turnips pre-chopped in a plastic bag, but I think the whole ones are fresher. I chop whole turnips into small bits, and use about 1 tablespoon per portion.

DRIED SHRIMPS (OPTIONAL): The cheaper versions of Pad Thai on the streets of Bangkok are made with only tiny dried prawns and no fresh prawns at all. I don't want to go that far, but I still like to add a little of these salty dried prawns for extra flavor. You can easily skip them altogether if you prefer. I take a bit of dried shrimps and pound it in a pestle and mortar until fluffy. It's important to use the mortar here and not your food processor, which will turn dried shrimps into hard, dried chunks (entirely capable of cracking a tooth) instead of fluffy salty bits. I use about 1 to 2 tablespoons per portion.

CHOPPED GARLIC (OPTIONAL): I like to use a little bit of garlic in each portion, to give it an extra kick. You don't have to.

To serve as condiments at the table you will need lime wedges (one per each portion), extra ground peanuts, extra chili powder, fish sauce, and even a bit of white sugar. As with other street food in Thailand, everyone can tailor the final dish to taste. I suggest a squeeze of lime for sure, and anything else that pleases you.

Cooking the Pad Thai

Follow these steps carefully and the best Pad Thai you've ever had will be the one you've just made. Keep the pot of sauce warm on another burner next to your wok and have a bowl of water handy too. That way, if things get too hot in the wok you can sprinkle the water onto it to slow it down.

1. Heat a large wok over high heat until very hot, to the point of smoking.

2. Add about 3 to 4 tablespoons of vegetable oil. Don't be shy. This isn't no diet food.

3. Add the protein you are using (chicken, peeled prawns, or whole prawns). Stir vigorously, until it's halfway cooked, about 1 to 2 minutes. Add 2 tablespoons of sauce to flavor, and a pinch of garlic (if using). Add the tofu. Cook for another minute until the protein is done and the tofu is crisp and slightly brown at the edges. Transfer to a bowl and set aside.

4. Add the noodles and then about ¼ cup/55ml of warm sauce. Stir vigorously, keeping everything moving in the wok, and cook the noodles until they are soft. Remember to break up the noodles and don't let them clump together. If the sauce evaporates too quickly and your noodles aren't quite ready, sprinkle a bit of water on them and keep stirring. Add a bit of oil if the noodles still stubbornly stick together.

5. When the noodles are ready (taste them to be sure), push them up to one side of the wok and crack an egg into the middle. Let it set for 10 to 15 seconds and toss everything all together.

6. Add the pickled turnips, ground peanuts, ground prawns, and bean sprouts. Stir well after each addition. Add more sauce if it looks a little pale.

7. Add the reserved protein back to the wok. Stir quickly to combine. Add a handful of garlic chives. Turn the heat off, and quickly give the wok a good stir to mix everything together.

8. Place the finished Pad Thai on a plate and serve to your first lucky dinner guest. Give the used wok a quick rinse with warm water, and wipe off any excess bits of food with a warm towel. Place the wok back over a high heat and add the oil.

9. As soon as it heats back up to smoking, you're ready to do another portion. Repeat this process until all your dinner guests have been served. Keep them lubricated and happy with ample supplies of Riesling, Champagne, or beer while they wait. That's how I do it!

Salads

I believe you become a true foodie when you stop buying bottled salad dressing. Once you master the basic salad dressing ingredients – vinegar, oil, salt, and pepper – you can combine them into countless variations. Making a dressing from scratch takes just a few minutes, and I don't even dirty another bowl, as I make the dressing right in the salad bowl.

For my favorite everyday dressing, I start with vinegar and a bit of finely chopped shallot. I add a bit of mustard and a tiny dab of mild honey, and then sprinkle in salt and a bit of pepper. I mix the ingredients well, incorporating everything before whisking in the oil last. That's all. I don't really measure anything, except I usually start with the basic proportion of two spoons of vinegar to four spoons of oil. I change the size of the spoon to fit the quantity of salad I plan to toss. For a single portion for myself I use a dessertspoon to measure, then change to a soupspoon for two, and perhaps a big wooden spoon I use to toss a large salad bowl for a crowd. I use more or less vinegar depending on what kind of vinegar I use and how sharp I want the dressing to be.

You can experiment with different oils and vinegars. I often have at least three or four different vinegars on hand, including basic white wine (or Champagne) and red wine vinegars, sherry vinegar, and rice vinegar. For more subtle vinaigrettes I would use white wine or Champagne vinegar. Red wine vinegar provides a more robust,

sharper tone, and I use sherry vinegar for just a hint of sweetness. In winter, when fragrant citrus such as lemons and mandarins are in season, I like to use them in place of vinegar.

Taste a variety of olive oils and keep one or two that you like on hand. If you like lighter-tasting oil, try Arbequina oil from Spain or Taggiasca oil from Liguria. For fuller-bodied oil, try Picual oil from Spain, the robust oils from Tuscany or Sicily, or the Tuscan-style olive oils from Northern California.

Once you expand your horizon beyond olive oil, there's a whole other world of oils to explore. I love using hazelnut or walnut oils to accent my vinaigrette. I always keep subtle oil such as light olive or grapeseed oil on hand. I use them to balance and lighten the sometimes overwhelming power of the nut oil. There is such a thing as too much of a good thing in this case.

Try the combination of these two nut oils in your vinaigrette, and you will love it as much as I do. It makes a nearly instant sauce for a quick weekday dinner. For example, you can drizzle it over a piece of pan-fried fish.

Salad of mesclun and tatsoi flowers with nut oil vinaigrette

This salad uses the yellow flowers from *tatsoi*, a variety of Chinese mustard green. Tatsoi flowers have a wonderfully nutty flavor that combines beautifully with the accents from the nut oils in the dressing. You can replace tatsoi with any edible flowers you can find, or skip them altogether.

SERVES 4

few handfuls small green-leaf lettuce and other greens, such as tatsoi and
     Chinese mustard greens

VINAIGRETTE
1 teaspoon mustard
salt
2 tablespoons sherry vinegar
3 tablespoons olive oil *
2 tablespoons walnut oil
1 tablespoon hazelnut oil
freshly ground black pepper

Assemble a mix of small green-leaf lettuce and any other greens you like. In another large salad bowl, add the mustard, a pinch of salt, and vinegar. Mix well with the back of a wooden spoon or a whisk. In a small bowl, combine the three kinds of oil and stir quickly to mix. Pour the mixed oils into the salad bowl in a thin stream while whisking or stirring vigorously to emulsify the dressing. Grind over some black pepper and add more salt if needed. Place the greens into the bowl with the vinaigrette and toss until the leaves are thoroughly coated.

*Use very light Ligurian or Catalan olive oil for this recipe. If you only have robust, Tuscan-style olive oil, use only 2 tablespoons and substitute the third with grapeseed oil.

Soups

Strawberry "gazpacho"

Recipe adapted from David Kinch

David makes this delightful summer soup that hides a surprise, replacing the classic tomatoes with strawberries. Visually it looks just like a traditional red gazpacho, but the flavor is refreshingly original. Sometimes I give in to my classical side and substitute half the amount of strawberries with juicy, ripe tomatoes. It makes just as delicious a soup, if a tad less daring, for a hot summer's day.

SERVES 6 to 8

GAZPACHO

1lb | 500g strawberries, hulled and lightly crushed
4oz | 110g white onions, thinly sliced
4oz | 110g red peppers, thinly sliced
5oz | 150g cucumber, peeled, seeded, thinly sliced
1/2 garlic clove, crushed
2 stems of fresh tarragon, leaves picked
1/4 cup | 55ml balsamic vinegar
1/4 cup | 55ml extra-virgin olive oil
salt and pepper

strawberries, hulled and finely diced
small handful of fresh chives, finely minced
3oz | 75g red pepper, finely diced
1/4 cup | 110g finely diced English cucumber, peeled and deseeded
1 to 2 tablespoons almond oil
whole sprigs of fresh chervil

Place all the gazpacho ingredients except the salt and pepper in a bowl. Mix well and cover with plastic wrap. Refrigerate for a few hours or overnight.

The next day, purée the ingredients in a blender and season with salt and pepper to taste. If the mixture is too thick, add water to thin it down. Allow the soup to chill again before ladling it into soup plates or bowls.

To finish, gently toss all the garnish ingredients with the almond oil. Place them in a mound in the centre of the soup dish and top with some chervil sprigs.

You can serve this soup in a clear glass to show off the layers. Place the garnished ingredients (except the chervil) at the bottom of the glass, pour the gazpacho over it and top with the chervil.

Roasted squash soup with brown butter

SERVES 6 to 7

1 medium-sized blue or hubbard or buttercup squash, weighing about 3¹/4lb/1.5kg
2 teaspoons unsalted butter
2 tablespoons light brown sugar
sea salt

1 cup | 250g unsalted butter, cubed
2 cups | 400ml vegetable or chicken stock
pinch of cayenne pepper
1/4 teaspoon ground cinnamon
1/4 teaspoon ground nutmeg
pinch of allspice
splash of white wine vinegar
splash of freshly squeezed lemon juice
salt

Cut the squash in half, and remove the strings and seeds. Line a baking sheet with aluminium foil and place the squash on it, cut-side up. Place about a teaspoon of butter, a tablespoon of brown sugar, and a pinch of salt into the center of each half. Roast until the squash is completely soft, about 1 hour. The top of the squash should brown up nicely, but cover them with foil if they are threatening to go from brown to burned. When they are finished remove them from the oven and let them stand until cool.

While the squash is cooling down, make a brown butter. Place the cubed butter in a small saucepan over medium heat until it has completely melted. Continue cooking until the butter boils, at which point it will foam up. Wait until the foam begins to subside. When the butter takes on a golden hazelnut color, remove it from the heat immediately. Strain the butter into another bowl and set it aside to cool.

Scrape the flesh of the squash from the skin. Add the flesh and the stock to a blender and process until smooth. Add the brown butter and continue until emulsified. Then add the spices, a tiny splash each of vinegar and lemon juice and a pinch of salt. Blend again to combine.

Pour the soup into a medium-sized saucepan. Correct the seasoning as necessary. Reheat the soup until it is just warm enough to serve, but don't allow it to come to a full boil as the butter emulsion will break. This is a very rich soup, and a small portion goes a long way.

Fish

I can see why a lot of new cooks are afraid of cooking fish. It's not easy to find great-quality fish in regular markets, and even harder to find whole fish. Things are, happily, changing for the better, I used to have to trek over to Chinatown to buy whole fish, but now my local Whole Foods sometimes carries fresh whole red snapper.

When I can get fresh whole fish, I stuff the middle with slices of lemon and any herbs I have on hand, and drizzle all over it with good olive oil. I bake the fish in a 400°F/200°C/Gas Mark 6 oven for about 20 to 30 minutes or until it's done, and serve with a sharp vinaigrette to drizzle on top.

When I'm in the mood to do something extra-special, I use the following recipes.

Sea bass with artichokes, tomatoes, fennel, and olives
Recipe adapted from Yannick Alleno

This is my favorite summer dish at Yannick Alleno's three-star restaurant Le Meurice, in Paris. At Le Meurice, Yannick uses beautiful Mediterranean *rouget de roche* (red mullet) for the dish. At home, perfectly fresh mullet are hard to come by and – trust me – you don't want to work with less than pristine mullet, so I often use fresh sea

bass instead. The beauty of this recipe is that you can make it as simple or as complicated as you like. If you are in the mood to do something fancy, follow the steps closely, and you too can make a three-star dish at home. If you want something quicker, you can easily cook all the vegetables together in the same pan and end up with a dish that is perhaps less refined but every bit as delicious.

SERVES 4

GRECQUE DE LEGUMES (GREEK-STYLE VEGETABLES)
1lb | 500g tomatoes
olive oil
1 tablespoon sugar
salt
4 medium-sized artichokes
juice of ¹/2 lemon
2 fennel bulbs
small handful of Chinese celery or leafy celery
1 large onion
2 garlic cloves, peeled
1 teaspoon fennel seeds
black pepper
splash of pastis (optional)
¹/4 cup | 55ml white wine
¹/2 cup | 120ml chicken or vegetable stock
¹/4 cup | 25g pitted black olives, sliced into rounds
1 tablespoon preserved lemon, cut into small cubes
1 sprig basil, leaves chopped

FISH
¹/4 cup | 55ml olive oil
4 sea bass filets, about 4oz | 110g each
fleur de sel
black pepper

PREHEAT THE OVEN TO: *200°F | 90°C | Gas Mark ¹/4*

Prepare the Grecque de legumes by peeling and seeding the tomatoes and then cutting each one into eight wedges. Lay the wedges on a large

HOW TO COOK LIKE A FOODIE

gratin dish, shower generously with $^1/_4$ cup/60ml of olive oil, add the sugar, and sprinkle with salt. Bake in the preheated oven for $2^1/_2$ hours. Set aside to cool. If you don't want to spend $2^1/_2$ hours baking the tomatoes, you can simply cook the tomato pieces in a small pan on the stove – cover them with olive oil until they are submerged, add the sugar, and season with salt. Cook over low heat, turning the pieces frequently. By the time everything else is prepared and ready, the tomatoes will be as well. When they are cooked, strain and set aside the now perfumed oil for another use, such as the next time you dress a salad.

To prepare the artichokes, add 4 cups/1 litre of cold water and the lemon juice to a medium-sized pot. Meanwhile, clean the artichokes by pulling away the outer leaves, then, with a paring knife, peel the remaining tough green skin until you are left with just the pale, soft artichoke hearts. Cut each heart into quarters, removing the fuzzy choke from the middle using the knife. Drop the cleaned artichokes into the pot with water and lemon (the lemon juice helps prevent them from discoloring).

Prepare the rest of the vegetables. Cut the roots and the green top from the fennel bulbs. Remove the tough outermost layer and cut the bulbs lengthwise into medium-thick slices. Cut the celery into thin sticks, $^1/_4$ inch/0.5cm wide and about $1^1/_2$ to 2 inches/4 to 5cm long. Peel and cut the onion into thin half-moon pieces.

Place a frying pan over medium-high heat. Add 1 to 2 tablespoons of olive oil, then the garlic cloves, onion, and fennel. Toss well and cook until the onion is translucent, then add the fennel seeds. Drain the artichokes and add them too. Season with salt and pepper, and continue to cook for another couple of minutes.

Add a splash of pastis (if using) and the white wine and let everything come to a full boil and cook for another minute after that. Then add the chicken or vegetable stock to the pan along with the celery and olives and turn the heat down to medium-low and let everything gently cook until the vegetables are just tender. Add the preserved lemon and the tomatoes. Taste and add more salt and pepper as needed. Remove the pan from the heat, sprinkle over the chopped basil leaves and set the vegetables aside until you are ready to serve.

Heat a frying pan over medium heat until hot. Add a liberal amount of the olive oil – just enough to coat the pan. Put the fish pieces, skin-side down, into the pan. Don't move the fish at all. Let them cook for a few minutes. Watch the sides of the fish; when the bottom half of the flesh turns opaque – it should only take a few minutes – gently flip the fish over to cook the other side. Cook for a couple more minutes until the fish is cooked to your liking. Sprinkle with good fleur de sel and a few turns of the peppermill.

Divide the vegetables between four plates and place one piece of fish on each one. Pour the juice from the pan over each piece of fish. Serve immediately.

Monkfish with "smoked" potato and mustard sauce
Recipe adapted from Alain Passard

SERVES 4

SMOKED POTATOES
10oz | 300g new potatoes
few pinches of salt
1 tablespoon butter, plus 1/2 tablespoon
2 to 3 cups | 500 to 750ml brewed lapsang souchong or smoked oolong tea

MUSTARD SAUCE
3 shallots, finely chopped
salt
2 tablespoons butter
about 1/2 cup | 110ml white wine
3 tablespoons vermouth
1/4 cup | 55ml fish stock (substitute water if you don't have fish stock on hand)
3/4 cup | 200ml cream
1/2 tablespoon mustard (Alain uses Moutarde d'Orleans)
black pepper
squeeze of lemon juice (optional)

MONKFISH
1 tablespoon butter
1 tablespoon olive oil
4 pieces of monkfish, about 5oz | 150g each; (If you can't find sustainably caught monkfish, you can use other light, white-fleshed fish, such as halibut or sea bass instead.)

Put the potatoes in a pot of water over medium heat. Add a few pinches of salt and the 1 tablespoon of butter. Allow to simmer until the potatoes are cooked through. Then, drain the potatoes, peel them and place them in a large bowl. Pour the brewed souchong tea over them and let them soak for 5 to 10 minutes, depending on the smokiness of your lapsang. You want the potatoes to pick up a slightly smoky nose from it, but not overwhelmingly so. Drain the potatoes, discard the tea, and toss the remaining 1/2 tablespoon of butter into the "smoked" potatoes. Set them aside in a warm place until you are ready to serve them.

Put the finely chopped shallots into a shallow dish. Sprinkle some salt over them and set aside for 15 to 20 minutes. Place a frying pan over low heat and add the 2 tablespoons of butter. Add the chopped shallots and let them gently sweat until they are translucent and soft, taking care not to let them discolor. Pour in the white wine. Turn the heat up high and cook until nearly all the wine evaporates, leaving only a syrupy liquid on the pan. Add the vermouth and let this cook for about a minute to allow the alcohol to evaporate. Add the fish stock (or water) and boil it until it reduces to a syrupy consistency. Turn the heat down to low again, add the cream and let it gently simmer until it reduces to a beautiful silky sauce. Strain it into a medium-sized bowl and whisk in the mustard. Check the seasoning of the sauce and add pepper and a bit of salt if needed. If the sauce is too salty at this point, add a squeeze of lemon juice to bring it back into balance. Keep the sauce warm while you attend to the fish.

Put a pan large enough to accommodate the four pieces of fish on the stove over medium heat. When the pan is hot, add the butter and olive oil. Arrange the fish pieces in the pan and let them cook undisturbed for 2 minutes. Keep your eyes on the side of the fish, and when you can see the bottom half of the flesh turning opaque, flip the fish and continue to cook on the other side for another couple of minutes, until cooked. Inserting a toothpick in the middle of the fish will tell you if it is done or not; a cooked piece of fish will let the toothpick through easily, while fish that is still raw will put up some resistance.

To serve, place a piece of fish in each plate. Divide the potatoes evenly between them. Spoon the warm sauce generally over the fish and the potatoes.

Sea bass and poached artichokes in mandarin–olive oil emulsion

When my friend Mikael first cooked this dish for us when we were on vacation in the south of France, he used beautiful thorny *épine* artichokes we had bought from a local market. I was duly impressed. I'd never seen artichokes before with those big, sharp thorns. They are vindictive too – and this is from first-hand experience trimming them. However, you can use just about any type of artichoke you can find at your local market. Just make sure they are in season, and use the ones that are young and tender. Big, old, woody artichokes are just not worth the effort.

You can serve the artichokes on their own (double or triple the quantity as needed) in the mandarin and olive oil emulsion as the first course in a multicourse dinner, or use the full recipe with the fish to serve as a main course.

SERVES 4

ARTICHOKES
3 cups | 700ml of water
1/2 tablespoon salt
juice of 1/2 lemon
6 to 8 artichokes, trimmed and quartered

FISH
salt
4 sea bass fillets, about 4oz | 120g each, preferably with skin on
*   and at room temperature*
3 tablespoons olive oil

SAUCE
juice of 1 to 2 mandarin oranges or 1 large orange
pinch of salt
6 tablespoons very good extra-virgin olive oil*
squeeze of lemon juice (optional)
black pepper

In a small saucepan add the water, salt, and lemon juice and bring the liquid to a boil. Add the prepared artichokes. Poach for 6 to 8 minutes over a low heat. Start checking if the artichokes are cooked at about 6 minutes: the tip of a knife should go into an artichoke without any resistance once it is ready. When cooked, turn off the heat, strain the artichokes, and set them aside.

Heat a frying pan – a non-stick pan will be easier to work with – until it is medium-hot. Sprinkle a little salt on both sides of the fish fillets. Add the olive oil to the hot pan, so that it is well coated. Arrange the fillets in the pan, skin-side down, and let them cook undisturbed for 2 minutes or until the skin underneath is lovely and golden brown.

Turn the fillets over and continue to cook for 2 to 3 minutes. Test whether the fish is ready by using a cake tester or toothpick – it should go in and come out with no resistance when the fish is done. If you don't have a cake tester, you can straighten out a metal paper clip and use that instead.

While the fish is cooking you can make a quick sauce. Begin by adding a pinch of salt to 3 tablespoons of the mandarin juice. Using a whisk, or a fork if you're good, slowly mix the juice into the olive oil, whisking constantly to create an emulsion. Add more mandarin juice if the sauce is not sharp enough, or even a squeeze of lemon. Finish with a few turns of black pepper.

When the fish is cooked, take the fillets out of the pan and place each on warm plates to serve. Arrange a few pieces of artichoke on each of the plates, and then pour a couple of tablespoons of the mandarin–olive oil emulsion on top of the artichokes and around the sea bass. Serve immediately.

*The best oil for this recipe is low-acid olive oil made from ripe olives. The greenish Tuscan-style olive oil, which tends to be from olives that are not fully ripe, will not work as well here. Instead, use Ligurian oils from Italy or Catalan oils from around Barcelona. Spanish olive oils are also generally lower in acid than the Californian or Tuscan varieties.

Baked sole with exotic spices
Recipe adapted from Olivier Roellinger

This recipe came from Olivier Roellinger, a famous chef from Brittany, France. He has a reputation of deftly using exotic spices to enhance his cuisine. This dish is a perfect example of this, with a delicate and expert use of spices to heighten the flavor without overwhelming the fish. It is a wonderful dish to herald the arrival of spring, using new potatoes, delicate baby leeks or spring onions, and fresh sole. But you hardly need to limit yourself to the one season. The recipe is easily adapted to warm you on a cool autumn evening or even in front of a winter fire (or the video of a crackling fire you've got running on TV in your city apartment).

Use other white-fleshed fish if you can't find sole. Halibut, plaice, or monkfish will work just fine here. Use regular leeks if the season isn't right for delicate young shoots of leeks, or regular-sized potatoes (the waxy variety like Charlotte or Ratte) instead of the small ones. Just cut them down into smaller chunks.

SERVES 4

GRAINES LOINTAINES (FARAWAY SPICES) SAUCE
3 | 15g whole hazelnuts
3 | 15g whole almonds
2 teaspoons sesame seeds
1 teaspoon coriander seeds
^{1}/2 teaspoon sumac
1 teaspoon cumin seeds
3oz | 75g butter
fish bones
zest of 1 orange
zest of 1 lemon
1 tablespoon lemon juice (or more to taste)
1 cup | 225ml chicken stock
2 garlic cloves, peeled

20 baby leeks or 3 to 4 small leeks
10oz | 300g new potatoes
6 tablespoons | 80g butter
salt
4 skinless sole fillets, about 4oz/110g each (ask your fishmonger to reserve some
of the bones for you)
black pepper

TO SERVE: *Bread*

First prepare a spice mix. In a small pan over medium heat, toast the hazelnuts and almonds until they are fragrant and slightly brown. Transfer the nuts to a plate and place in the freezer. Add the sesame, coriander, sumac, and cumin to the pan. Toast them all for a few more minutes, tossing frequently, until everything is fragrant. Remove from the heat, transfer to a plate and let cool to room temperature.

When the spices are at room temperature, take the nuts out of the freezer and roughly chop them with a knife. Add the chopped nuts and the spices to a mortar, and grind the mixture into a fine powder. Transfer the spice mix to a jar and cover tightly until ready to use.

To make the sauce, heat a large frying pan over medium-high heat. Add the butter and then the fish bones. Cook for a few minutes to brown, basting the bones frequently with the butter. Add 1 tablespoon of the spice mix to the pan and continue to cook. After 1 minute, add the orange and lemon zests, and the lemon juice and let cook for another minute. Then add the chicken stock and the garlic cloves and let everything simmer on a very low heat. After 30 minutes remove the pan from the heat and strain the liquid. Discard the fish bones and garlic. At this point the sauce should have a consistency somewhere between milk and heavy cream. If the sauce is too thick, add a bit of water to thin it out. If it's too thin, turn the heat up to high to quickly reduce the sauce to a proper consistency.

While the sauce is simmering, you can be preparing the leeks and the potatoes. If using baby leeks, trim the roots and cut two 1½-in/4-cm pieces from the bottom, and discard the green tops. If using regular leeks, trim the roots and the green part from the leeks and discard them. Cut lengthwise through the middle of the leeks and rinse off any dirt that may be trapped inside. Cut the leeks on the bias into thin slices and set aside. Peel and wash the potatoes. Chef Roellinger suggests rubbing the surface of the potatoes with large grains of salt, but you certainly can skip this step.

Preheat the oven to 400°F/200°C /Gas Mark 6. Place the potatoes and 1 tablespoon/10g of the butter in a small pot. Then add enough water to cover. Add salt until the water tastes salty. Bring to a boil and cook until the potatoes are just barely done. This could take from 10 minutes to nearly half an hour, depending on the size and type of potatoes you use. Cook until you are able to insert the tip of a knife through the flesh with only a little resistance.

While the potatoes are cooking, quickly sweat the leeks in a little bit of butter in a frying pan, for just a minute or two until they are nearly translucent but not completely cooked. Tip the leeks onto a plate and set aside. Rinse the pan and return it to the stove.

Heat the pan over medium-high heat until quite hot. Season the fish generously with salt. Melt the remaining butter in the pan, and then add the fish. Sear the fillets quickly to brown them lightly on both sides. The fish doesn't need to be thoroughly cooked right now because it will finish cooking in the oven with the sauce.

Arrange the cooked potatoes and leeks in a large baking or casserole dish. Place the fish fillets over them. Pour the sauce over everything and place the dish in the preheated oven. After 10 minutes, check if the fish is cooked through. If not, put the dish back in the oven for a few more minutes until done. Remove from the oven and taste the sauce again to check the seasoning. Add more salt if needed. Finish with a few turns of the peppermill.

Serve in the baking dish or divide between four plates. Be sure to get every little bit of the sauce onto the plates, as your guests will want every last drop for their bread.

Any leftover spice mix will keep in the fridge in an airtight jar for a month.

Meat

Braised leg of lamb with young onions

Recipe adapted from Alain Chapel

Alain Chapel was an inspiration to an entire generation of chefs, from
the avant garde Heston Blumenthal to the classicist Michel Roux, and
Alain Ducasse. Thomas Keller and David Kinch cited a meal at his
restaurant in the village of Mionnay, in Lyon, as an epiphany and
turning point in their respective careers.

Alain Chapel's style was deceptively simple. The dish that changed
David's cooking life was a roasted pigeon served with peas and lettuce
from the restaurant's garden. This recipe is classic Alain Chapel: two
main ingredients, each coaxed to express the best quality of itself, combined
to create a deeply complex and flavorful dish. The technique here is also
genius. The blazing heat at the beginning draws out the fat to the surface,
allowing it to brown and caramelize properly during cooking later.

For this recipe, buy a small leg of spring lamb that weighs 5lb
(about 2.5kg). Any larger and the meat could be tough and not suitable
for this recipe. Use young spring onions with bright green stalks and
glossy, translucent skin. Serve this dish as a main course on a brisk
evening in early spring. Pull any leftover meat from the bone and use it to
make sandwiches for lunch the next day. It makes such a great sandwich
you might consider braising an entire leg just for sandwiches next time.

5lb | 2.5kg leg of lamb (Ask your butcher to cut off the excess bone so the leg
  fits your pan.)
salt
1/2 cup plus 3 tablespoons | 150g butter
3 1/4 lb | 1.5kg young spring onions
2 tomatoes
scant 1/4 cup | 40g sugar
2 cups | 500ml dry white wine
2 cups | 500ml beef or chicken stock or water
pepper

EQUIPMENT: *Large cast-iron or enamel pot, preferably oval in shape, or a*
large deep roasting pan; baster
PREHEAT THE OVEN TO: *500°F | 260°C | Gas Mark 10*

Cut 3 to 4 slashes through the top and bottom of the leg, and salt the
entire leg liberally. Cut 4 tablespoons/50g of the butter into large cubes
and set them in the roasting pan. Place the leg of lamb on top of the
butter and place the pan in the oven to roast. Meanwhile, prepare the
vegetables. Trim the spring onions to leave about 2 inches/5cm of
the green stalks attached to the onion bulbs for a pretty presentation.
Peel and seed the tomatoes and cut them into large chunks. Set the
vegetables aside.

   After 25 minutes take the lamb out of the oven. Turn the heat
down to 350°F/175°C /Gas Mark 5. Remove the leg of lamb from the
roasting pan and set it aside. Pour out the excess fat and butter at the
bottom of the pan. Add scant 1/4 cup/50g of butter, the sugar, and the spring
onions to the pan and toss well to coat the onions with the melting
butter. Put the pan on the stove over medium heat and continue to toss
the onions quickly to brown them, for about 2 to 3 minutes. When they
are well browned, place the leg of lamb back into the roasting pan on
top of the onions and return the pan to the oven.

   After 20 minutes, pull out the oven shelf that the pan is sitting
on as far as you can. Add the tomato chunks and the white wine
but be careful because they might spatter when they hit the hot pan.

Use a wooden spoon to scrape the brown bits from the bottom and baste the leg of lamb with the juices in the pan. Cover the pan loosely with a piece of foil, slide the shelf back in and close the oven.

Continue to cook for another 1½ to 2 hours, regularly turning and basting the leg with the juices. The liquid at the bottom of the pan should be slightly syrupy, but add a bit of stock to moisten it if the liquid reduces too quickly. You might not need to use the entire quantity of the stock specified in the ingredients list. The key is to keep the juice syrupy and baste the lamb regularly.

When the lamb is tender, after about 2 hours of cooking, take the roasting pan out of the oven. Remove the leg of lamb and set it aside to rest for at least 20 minutes before serving. Keep it warm, covered loosely with foil while it rests.

Put the pan on the stove over medium heat, add the rest of the butter, a few turns of the peppermill and shake the pan well to mix. You may add a bit more of the stock if the juice is too thick. Check the seasoning, and add more salt or pepper if needed. If the juice is too salty add a splash of vinegar – any kind from the cupboard will do.

To serve, place the leg of lamb on a serving platter, smothered with the onions and sauce.

Grilled rack of lamb with fresh herbs

The best grilled rack of lamb ever. Try it and you will believe me.

SERVES 4

¹/4 cup | 55ml olive oil
¹/4 cup plus 1 tablespoon | 60g salted butter, melted
5 sprigs of fresh rosemary
2 half racks of lamb, each holding 8 bones (ask your butcher to "french" the
racks and remove the chine bones for you)
sea salt
2 tablespoons each chopped fresh thyme, mint, and flat leaf parsley, plus
1 teaspoon finely chopped fresh rosemary, mixed

EQUIPMENT: *Kitchen twine, meat thermometer*

You can cook the lamb on a gas barbecue or a wood fire. For the gas barbecue, use the lowest setting possible. For the wood fire, let the flames burn all the way down until only white embers remain before cooking.

Mix the olive oil and melted butter. Take a length of kitchen twine and tie the sprigs of rosemary together at one end to form a brush. Using the rosemary sprigs, brush both racks of lamb with the olive oil and butter mixture. Do not add salt yet.

Slowly cook the racks of lamb over the grill, turning them every so often to slowly cook on all sides. Baste occasionally with the olive oil and butter mixture, using the rosemary brush. This process is not difficult, but it is lengthy and requires attention. It will take about 45 minutes to cook the lamb to perfectly pink and rare inside, so grab a glass of wine to enjoy while doing this. A few companions for a good chat will be even better.

In about 45 minutes the lamb should be cooked to rare, about 130°F/55°C internal temperature. If you like the lamb done a bit more, continue to cook until the thermometer inserted into the thickest part of the rack reads 135° to 140°F/55° to 60°C, which will be medium-rare to medium. Any more done is inadvisable. Go to McDonald's instead.

When the lamb racks are cooked to the desired doneness, remove them from the heat. Sprinkle the racks with sea salt then shower them with the mixed fresh herbs until completely covered. Let them stand for 10 minutes to rest before serving in a pretty pan or dish.

Catalan surf & turf: braised chicken and prawns

I first found this recipe in Coleman Andrew's seminal book on Catalan cuisine called, simply, *Catalan Cuisine*. I love it so much, and make it all the time. The recipe is a classic Catalan ragout, with a base of what's called *sofregit*, a blend of onion and tomato cooked until caramelized. Then, to finish, it's thickened with what's basically a Catalan version of a roux called *picada* – made with fried bread, almond, chocolate, garlic, and parsley mashed together into a thick paste. It's a deliciously savory dish, comfort food with a little twist. Try it and I'm sure you'll make it just as often as I do. By the way, if you don't have a copy of that book yet, I highly suggest you get one.

SERVES 4

1/4 cup | about 55ml olive oil
4 to 5 lb | about 2 kg chicken, cut up into 8 pieces
8 to 12 large prawns (about 1 1/2 lb | 750g), preferably with shells and heads on
2 medium-sized onions (about 13 oz | 400g), diced
salt
10oz | 300g diced tomatoes (about 2 large tomatoes), peeled and seeded
1 piece of bread (about 1oz | 25g), crust removed
1oz | 25g dark chocolate, chopped
4 garlic cloves (about 3/4 oz | 20g), peeled
8 almonds (about 1/2 oz | 12g)
4 sprigs of fresh parsley
1/2 cup | 110ml dry white wine
splash of Pernod

In a deep saucepan (or 1¹/₂ gallon/8 quart Dutch oven), heat 3 tablespoons of oil until hot. Brown the chicken pieces on both sides. Do this in two batches so you don't crowd the pan and the chicken pieces color properly. Set the chicken aside. Add the prawns and cook them quickly until nicely red on both sides. Set the prawns aside.

Lower the heat and in the same pan add the diced onions and a big pinch of salt. Cook the onions until translucent and caramelized – about 5 minutes. Add the diced tomatoes, another pinch of salt and continue cooking for 5 more minutes, until the tomato chunks break down and almost "melt" into the onions. This is referred to as the *sofregit* in Catalan cuisine.

Arrange the chicken pieces over the bed of onion and tomato sofregit. Sprinkle some salt over the chicken. Add 3 cups/600ml of water to the pan. Turn the heat to high and bring to a boil. Turn the heat back down to a simmer and continue to cook for 20 minutes, with the lid off.

While the chicken is cooking, make your *picada*. In a small frying pan, heat the rest of the oil until hot. Add the bread and fry until brown on both sides. In a small food processor or blender, add the chopped chocolate, garlic cloves, almonds, and the fried bread. Remove the leaves from two sprigs of parsley and add to the processor. Add a little liquid from the chicken pan to just moisten the mix and blend until fine. Set aside.

After the 20 minutes, add the white wine and a big splash of Pernod to the chicken. Turn the heat to high and bring it back to the boil. Then turn the heat down again and simmer for 10 to 15 minutes, or until the chicken pieces are cooked through and tender. After that, add the prawns back to the pan and stir in the picada. Taste it, you might need to add more salt. Cover with a lid and simmer for five more minutes. Remove the stems from the remaining parsley and chop the leaves finely, and sprinkle over the dish before serving.

Prune and root vegetable stew

This elegant vegetable recipe is a simplified version of a dish David serves at Manresa and makes a perfect accompaniment for roast meat.

SERVES 4 to 6

1/2 cup | 50g pitted prunes
1 cup strong, brewed black tea
5oz | 150g black radishes or turnips, peeled and cut into bite-sized pieces
1 cup chicken stock or vegetable stock
1 tablespoon soy sauce
3 tablespoons | 40g unsalted butter
5oz | 150g baby carrots, quartered lengthwise
salt and black pepper
5oz | 150g fingerling potatoes
1 small onion, finely chopped

1 large garlic clove, finely chopped
5oz | 150g Jerusalem artichokes, peeled and cut into ¹/₂-inch | 1-cm wedges
1 bay leaf
1 sprig of fresh thyme
2 sprigs of fresh parsley
juice of ¹/₄ lemon

EQUIPMENT: *Large enamel cast-iron casserole*
PREHEAT THE OVEN TO: *400°F | 200°C | Gas Mark 6*

In a small saucepan, cover the prunes with the tea and bring to a simmer. Remove from the heat, cover, and let stand until the prunes are plump, about 1 hour. Drain the prunes and discard the tea.

In a medium saucepan, cover the radishes with the chicken stock and soy sauce and bring to a boil. Simmer over medium heat for about 10 minutes or until the radishes are tender. Drain them, but reserve the cooking liquid.

Meanwhile, melt 2 tablespoons of the butter in a frying pan. Add the carrots and season with salt and pepper. Cook over a medium heat, stirring for about 2 minutes. Add enough water to cover the carrots by 1 inch/2.5cm and bring to a boil. Simmer over moderate heat for about 7 minutes or until tender, then drain.

In a large enameled cast-iron casserole, melt the remaining tablespoon of butter. Add the potatoes and cook over medium heat for about 8 minutes, stirring, until they are tender and golden. Add the onion and cook for about 4 minutes or until softened. Stir in the garlic and cook for about 1 minute or until fragrant.

Add the prunes, carrots, Jerusalem artichokes, the radishes with their cooking liquid, and the herbs and season with salt and pepper. Roast in the oven for 15 minutes or until the vegetables are tender and the liquid is slightly reduced. Remove from the oven, finish with lemon juice, and serve.

Rice and noodles

Risotto with saffron and licorice powder

Adapted from Massimiliano Alajmo, Le Calandre, Italy

This beautiful risotto is a perfect showcase of the ingenious whimsy of Massimiliano Alajmo of Le Calandre, near Padova, in Italy. I have to warn you, saffron and licorice are both strongly flavoured, and the combination is quite striking. Try it when you're in a daring enough mood. You might never go back to regular risotto again.

SERVES 4

3¹/₂ pints | 2 litres chicken stock
couple pinches of saffron
1 tablespoon extra-virgin olive oil
1¹/₂ cups | 325g carnaroli rice
¹/₂ medium-sized | 50g onion, finely diced
¹/₃ cup | 75ml white wine
salt
4¹/₂ tablespoons | 60g butter
³/₄ cup | 75g grated Parmesan cheese
1 tablespoon lemon juice
small stick of licorice root for garnish (found in health food stores)

Warm the chicken stock in a pot over low heat. Add a pinch of saffron to the broth and let it simmer while you start on the rice.

In a saucepan or a deep frying pan, add the oil and toast the rice over medium heat, shaking the pan from time to time, for a few minutes until the grains are translucent. Add the onion, stir it through the rice and cook until translucent. Add the wine, stir well to mix, then let it cook until most of the wine is evaporated. Add another pinch of saffron and a pinch of salt.

Begin adding the warmed chicken stock, one ladle at a time. Stir until the liquid thickens again before adding another ladle. Continue until the stock is used up and the rice is soft on the outside but teetering at the edge of being underdone. There should be enough liquid remaining in the risotto so the texture resembles wet rice pudding. Remove it from the heat and stir in the butter, Parmesan cheese, and lemon juice.

Spoon the risotto onto four plates and sprinkle or grate licorice over it. Licorice is so intensely flavored that I strongly suggest you err on the side of using not quite enough of it. That way you can always leave a licorice stick and grater at the table for your guests to add more if they would like.

If you want to be really fancy, take about two more cups of chicken broth and simmer that with a big pinch of saffron (or, less expensively, saffron powder). Reduce the liquid by two thirds, and you'll have a bright orange, enormously flavorful saffron reduction. Drizzle it, judiciously, on the finished risotto to add yet more color to the dish.

Khao soi: Northern Thai noodles with curry chicken

SERVES 4 to 6

CHICKEN CURRY
2 tablespoons vegetable oil
3 tablespoons | 75g red curry paste
2 teaspoons curry powder
1/2 teaspoon turmeric powder (optional)
1 brown (or black) cardamom, ground (optional)
3 cups | 700ml coconut milk

*3 to 4$^{1}/_{2}$ lb | 1.5 to 2kg chicken, cut into large pieces, or 2 legs, 2 thighs and
2 breast pieces, weighing about 3lb | 1.5kg in total*
fish sauce (nam pla), to taste
3 cups | 700ml chicken stock or water
$^{1}/_{2}$ teaspoon sugar

NOODLES
3 to 4 cups | 700ml to 1 litre vegetable oil, for frying
about 7 cups (loosely packed) Chinese bah-mi egg noodles

GARNISH
6 dried chiles
2 to 3 shallots, sliced very thinly
a large handful of Chinese pickled mustard greens, rinsed and thinly sliced
a handful of fresh coriander, chopped
3 limes, cut into wedges

EQUIPMENT: *Wok (or you can use a large frying pan)*

First make the chicken curry by heating a wok or heavy saucepan over
medium heat. When it is hot, add the oil, curry paste, curry powder, and
turmeric powder and ground cardamom (if using) and stir vigorously
to prevent the spices from burning. Cook for a few minutes until the
curry paste is fragrant.

Skim about 1 cup/225ml of the creamy part of coconut milk and
add it to the pan. Stir to mix well and continue to cook until you can see
a layer of red oil break from the paste. It is very important that you cook
this mixture until the oil starts to break out from the paste and you can
smell the aromatic spices.

Add the chicken and a few splashes of the fish sauce. Stir to coat
well, and let everything cook for about a minute or two. Then add the
rest of the coconut milk, plus about 1 cup/225ml of the chicken stock (or
water, if using). Lower the heat to simmering and cook until the
chicken is done. If the liquid reduces too quickly, add a little more water
or stock. The consistency of khao soi should be more like soup and not
sauce.

Add the sugar and check the seasoning. The flavor of the curry
should be salty and spicy, with a very slight aftertaste of sweetness.

When you taste the curry at this stage, it should be a bit saltier than what you would like the final dish to taste like. If it is under-salted now, the addition of the other ingredients at serving time will make it even more insipid, so you might need to add more fish sauce at this point.

While the chicken curry is simmering you can prepare the noodles and garnish. Line a plate with paper towels and set it aside. Place a wok or a frying pan over high heat. Pour in the oil until it is about 1inch/2.5cm deep, and heat it until it is very hot. Meanwhile, take one cup of the noodles (the remaining 6 cups will be used later) and fluff them up with a fork until the strands have separated.

When the oil is ready, sprinkle the noodles, a few at a time, into the pan. They will puff up immediately like an inflatable raft. Flip the noodle raft once. Cook the other side until it has browned evenly and then set it aside on the lined plate to drain the excess oil. Repeat this process until you finish frying the rest of the cup of noodles.

Add the dried chiles to the pan and stir them until they are well coated with oil. Be careful not to burn them. They cook very quickly so you need to remove them from the pan as soon as they puff up. Set them aside and remove the pan from the heat.

After the chicken curry is done remove it from the heat and set it aside to keep warm. Heat up a large pot of water to a full boil. Rinse the rest of the fresh noodles in cold water to wash out the excess starch. Drain, and add them to the very hot boiling water and cook for 2 to 3 minutes, stirring them well to prevent them from sticking.

When they are cooked, put some cooked noodles in a bowl, top with some curry, and garnish with the sliced shallots, pickled mustard greens and chopped coriander to taste. Take the browned fried noodles, lightly crush them and sprinkle some short strands on top as a garnish. Squeeze some lime juice over the curry just before eating, and add a fried chile if you want more heat.

HOW TO COOK LIKE A FOODIE

Clay-pot rice with lamb sausage and wild mushroom

David once commented that a meal wouldn't be complete without rice, and he's probably right. This earthy clay-pot rice recipe is a wonderful side dish, and it's even great just on its own.

Any leftovers can be cooked with several beaten eggs in a frying pan until it forms a crisp crust, then cut into wedges and served as a delicious, filling breakfast.

SERVES 8

4 cups | 300g about black trumpet mushrooms (or any wild mushroom you can find)
3 cups | 700ml mushroom stock*
salt
soy sauce
1lb | 450g lamb sausage meat
1^1/$_2$ cups | 325g Japanese short-grained rice

EQUIPMENT: Large clay pot about 6 to 7inches | 15 to 17cm in diameter and big enough to hold 3 pints | 2 litres
PREHEAT THE OVEN TO: 375°F | 190°C | Gas Mark 5

Clean the mushrooms by brushing off any dirt. If they are very soiled, rinse them quickly under running water, drain them well, and let them dry out for a bit on a tray lined with paper towels. Then slice them and set aside.

Put the stock in a stockpot and heat to a gentle boil. Taste the flavor of the stock carefully. Add a combination of salt and soy sauce until it is salty enough for your taste.

Meanwhile, heat a large frying pan over high heat until hot. Add the sausage meat to the pan, pressing it down lightly to form a thick patty on the pan. Let it cook until it is brown, then flip the patty over to brown the other side. When it is well browned all over, remove it from the pan with a slotted spoon and set it aside. Leave the remaining fat in the pan.

Turn the heat down to low and place the pan back on the stove. Pour the rice into it and stir it to coat all the grains well with the fat in the pan. Continue to cook and stir the rice grains in the pan until they are translucent, about 2 to 3 minutes.

Set a large clay pot on the stove over a low heat. Add the hot stock and the toasted rice. Stir, cover with the lid, and it let cook for 20 minutes until the rice is tender and the liquid absorbed. Turn the heat off.

While the rice is cooking, put the pan that was used for frying the rice back on the stove. Heat it until very hot, add the sliced mushrooms and fry them until they are brown. Remove them from the heat and set aside.

Break up the browned sausage patty into large chunks and add it to the clay pot. Add the browned mushrooms and mix gently to distribute the sausage chunks and the mushrooms well with the rice. Put the lid on the clay pot and place it in the preheated oven to bake.

After 30 minutes, remove the pot from the oven. Set it aside to rest for 10 minutes before serving. This will allow the crust that formed during the baking process to come out easily when served.

* If you don't have mushroom stock on hand, chicken stock or vegetable stock will do just as well. You can infuse mushroom flavor into your stock by adding the leftover trimmings of the mushrooms into the stockpot and letting it simmer until ready to use. Then strain the stock to remove the trimmings before adding the liquid into the clay pot with the rice.

Chorizo, eggs, and potatoes cooked in a cast-iron pan

David loves to say this is his Mexican-Californian twist on the classic Alpine breakfast, *rosti*. It's not exactly a rice or noodle dish, we often have it for breakfast served with tortillas, so I supposed it belongs here.

SERVES 8

1lb | 450g Mexican-style chorizo (fresh and without casing)
1 onion, finely chopped
1lb | 450g Charlotte potatoes, cooked, peeled, and cut into large chunks
salt
8 eggs
black pepper
chopped chives, to garnish

TO SERVE: *Good toasted bread or warm tortillas*
EQUIPMENT: *12-inch | 30-cm cast-iron frying pan*
PREHEAT THE OVEN TO: *325°F | 160°C | Gas Mark 3*

Set the cast-iron pan over medium heat. Add the chorizo, breaking it up with a wooden spoon. As soon as the fat begins to render from the meat, add the chopped onion. Continue to cook over medium heat until all the fat is rendered and the meat has cooked through. Remove the pan from the heat, and drain the cooked chorizo and onion into a colander placed over a large bowl to reserve the fat.

Put 2 tablespoons of the reserved fat back into the frying pan and place it over medium heat. Add the cooked potato chunks and a pinch of salt and fry until brown and crispy on all sides. Return the chorizo and onion to the frying pan, and mix them well with the potato. Spread the mixture evenly on the pan and then, using a wooden spoon, make eight indentations, about 1 inch/2.5cm deep, in the mixture. Crack an egg into each hole. Place the frying pan into the preheated oven for 6 to 8 minutes, or until the eggs are barely set with runny yolks. Remove the pan from the oven, season the eggs with a pinch of salt, pepper, and the chopped chives.

Serve with very good toasted bread or warm tortillas.

Pastry, sweet and savory

Frankly, I don't take people seriously when they tell me they can't bake. It's hardly rocket science. All you have to do is try it once. Baking is so satisfying and fun. Have a go, and learn how to make my very flakey tart dough, for example, and a whole world of fresh fruit tarts opens up for you. Trust me, try it, and you'll be baking a tart every weekend for the whole summer.

Basic tart dough
Makes enough for one open-faced 9-inch | 23-cm tart

PÂTE SABLÉE
1 cup plus 2 tablespoons | 125g plain flour
2 tablespoons | 25g sugar (optional)
$^1/_2$ cup | 110g unsalted cold butter
$^1/_2$ teaspoon salt
1 tablespoon cold milk (cold water will do at a pinch)

EQUIPMENT: *9-inch | 23-cm tart pan, pastry cutter*

Making the dough by hand

In a large bowl, blend the flour and sugar well with your fingers. Cut the cold butter into thin slices and put them on top of the mound of flour. Stir the pile of flour with your fingers to bury the butter slices into it.

Using a wire pastry blender, the tines of a fork, or just your fingers, press the butter into the flour until the dough is crumbly and the butter has broken up into pea-sized pieces. Work quickly so the butter doesn't melt too much, and don't worry if the bits of butter are not uniform in size.

Add the salt and drizzle in the milk mixing it in with your fingertips to distribute the liquid evenly. Coax the dough to come together to form a mass. Lightly knead the dough, pressing down with the heel of your hand and then folding the dough over itself. Repeat a few more times until you have cohesive dough. (Coat your fingers with a bit of flour if things get too sticky.) Put the dough between two sheets of plastic wrap and press it into a 4- to 5-inch/10- to 12-cm disc. Wrap it tightly and let rest for at least 2 hours or overnight before rolling it.

Making the dough in a food processor

Add the flour and sugar to your food processor and pulse them until they are blended. Cut the cold butter into large cubes and add them to the flour mixture. Pulse this a few times until the dough resembles moist and clumpy sand, with some larger bits of butter remaining. Add the salt then sprinkle the milk over the dough and pulse a few more times until the dough just begins to come together. Sprinkle a little bit of flour onto a dry work surface and empty the food processor onto it. Knead the dough with your hands quickly a few times, pressing down with the heel of your hand and then folding the dough over onto itself, until you have a ball of dough. Press this into a 4- to 5-inch/10- to 12-cm disc and wrap it tightly in plastic wrap. Let it rest in the fridge for an hour or overnight. You may also freeze the dough at this point to use later. It will keep for 3 months, just thaw it overnight in the fridge the day before you need to use it.

Once I have made my dough I prefer rolling it rather than pressing it into the pan by hand. Though it sounds easier, pressing creates a lot more mess, produces an uneven tart shell and, all in all, is a hassle. If you are afraid of the dough becoming too sticky to work, try rolling it in between two sheets of plastic wrap. Place your disc of dough in between two sheets large enough to cover the tart pan and roll the dough out to the desired size. This would be a large flat disc of dough that extends about 1^1/$_2$ inches/3.5cm over the rim of the tart pan all around. If your disc is a bit oblong, you might end up a bit short on one side, but you can easily use the excess dough to patch it later. And don't worry if there are a few tears. Just press the dough back together or patch it with a piece of excess dough. Peel one of the sheets of plastic wrap off and flip the dough onto the tart pan. Pick up the edges and push the hanging dough snugly down into the sides of the pan. Now peel off the other piece of plastic wrap, which should be on top of your tart pan at this time, and press the dough into the pan. Roll your rolling pin hard over the top of the tart to trim off the excess dough, and use the excess dough to patch any broken parts.

If you prefer to press the dough instead of rolling it, don't bother letting the dough rest before pressing into the pan. As you mix the butter, flour, and milk (in the machine or by hand), stop working the dough as soon as it is cohesive. Don't knead it. Instead, loosely distribute the dough, which will be fairly dry, evenly on the tart pan. Tear off a piece of plastic wrap large enough to cover the entire pan and lay it over the top of the dough. Using your fingertips or the heel of your hand, press down against the plastic wrap and pat the dough down to coat the bottom of the pan evenly. Press the dough into the corner and side of the pan, pushing down slightly from the top to create an even rim. Wrap tightly in plastic wrap around the pan and place it in the fridge to rest for 2 hours or overnight before using.

Very flaky pastry dough for pies and freeform tarts

This dough is incredibly sturdy, but bakes into a surprisingly tender dough. You will be astonished. It bakes up quite flaky, and works beautifully for a pie or a freeform tart. (For a tart shell baked in a tart pan I still prefer my regular pâte sablée recipe, page 116.) I actually came upon this recipe by mistake. While following Judy Rodger's (chef of Zuni Café in San Francisco) pastry dough recipe, I doubled everything else but forgot to double the amount of water. The resulting dough was supremely easy to work with. It can tolerate a lot of stretching and rolling, yet bakes into the lightest, flakiest, and most tender dough I've ever worked with. It's so great I came to refer to it as Magic Dough, and the mistake became my basic pastry dough recipe. After you have tried this once it will be yours too, I promise. This recipe makes two 10 inch/ 25cm open-face tarts, or one double-crust pie dough.

SERVES 6 to 8

1³/4 cups | 250g plain flour
1 cup | 225g salted butter
¹/4 cup | 55ml cold water

EQUIPMENT: *Pastry scraper*

Measure the flour onto a clean work surface. Cut the butter into large chunks and place them in one layer over the flour. Begin to blend the flour and butter together by pressing down on the pile with the heel of your hand. Using a pastry scraper held in your other hand, pick up some of the dough and flip it over the pile. Continue pressing and scraping up the dough until the butter resembles very thin flakes pressed into the flour.

Put down the pastry scraper and mix the dough with your fingertips until the flakes break up slightly, and the dough is now in a combination of big flakes and some crumbs.

Pour the cold water in thin stream into the dough, using your fingers to gently blend and distribute it evenly into the dough. Then start picking up the dough and pressing it on and over itself; using the pastry scraper here will help. Knead until you have a cohesive lump of dough. Gather it into a ball, press it down to a dish and wrap it tightly in plastic wrap. Let it rest in the fridge.

After 30 minutes, remove the dough from the fridge and roll it on a floured work surface. Stretch the dough out into a long rectangular shape, about 1 inch/2 to 3cm thick. Fold the dough in thirds toward the middle. Turn it 90 degrees and roll it out again to a rectangular shape, and fold again in thirds. Repeat this turning and rolling process a couple more times. When you are done, divide the dough in half and press each into a more or less round disk. Wrap each tightly in plastic wrap and store in the fridge. The dough should rest for at least another hour before use, or it can be frozen for up to a month.

Rustic fruit galette

You can use the very flaky pastry dough to make endless variations of rustic open-faced fruit galette. It's so easy I won't even call it a recipe. Just roll one dough disk into about a 10 to 12 inch/20 to 30cm round, smear about three tablespoons of Frangipane (below) all over by one inch in from the edge. Cut a few pieces of fruit (peaches, plums, apples, poached pears, whatever you want) and arrange them in a not-so-thick layer (and as artfully as you wish) on the dough. Fold the edges in, pinching a little to make sure they stick. If you want, you can brush the dough with eggwash and give it a good shower of sugar. Bake it in a preheated oven at 400°F/200°C/Gas Mark 6 for 45 minutes to an hour, until the crust is golden brown and the fruit caramelized.

Frangipane

Frangipane, the French almond paste used in many delicious pastries, is a very versatile recipe to have in your cooking arsenal. You can use it in fruit tarts, add it to cookie dough, or even stuff it into shop-bought croissants to make an easy but amazing breakfast treat.

Most frangipane recipes require almond paste, or almond flour, which can be difficult to find, not to mention quite expensive. My

recipe, adapted from that of legendary French chef, Michel Bras, starts with whole almonds, which you can find in supermarkets. Using whole almonds results in frangipane that's a little more rustic in texture, and I actually prefer it this way. I usually make a large portion because, wrapped tightly, it keeps very well in the freezer for spur-of-the-moment creations.

At the height of summer, when stone fruits like peaches and plums are at their ripest, I make freeform tarts, loading as much fruit as my pastry can handle. I spread a coating of frangipane at the bottom of the tart, using just enough to add a hint of nuttiness without overwhelming the flavor of the fruit. The frangipane also helps soak up and thicken the juice from the fruit pieces so the pastry stays crisp. In the autumn, I make a tart filled with nutty frangipane and cold-weather fruits like pears, quinces, or apples. A piece of tart served slightly warm, with a nice cup of tea or hot chocolate, is a lovely treat for a cold day. Add to that a good book and a cozy sofa and it's perfect. This quantity is enough for a 10-inch/25-cm tart or a number of freeform tarts.

SERVES 6 to 8

1/2 cup | *75g whole almonds*
1 1/4 oz | *35g granulated sugar*
1 1/4 oz | *35g confectioners' sugar (substitute granulated sugar here if you don't have confectioners' sugar on hand)*
3 oz | *75g butter, room temperature*
1 egg

PREHEAT THE OVEN TO: *350°F* | *180°C* | *Gas Mark 4*

Spread the almonds evenly on a baking sheet and place them in the oven. Roast them for about 10 to 12 minutes or until slightly toasted and fragrant. Transfer to a plate and let cool to room temperature.

Put the cooled almonds and the sugars into the bowl of a food processor and process until fine. Add the butter, and pulse a few times to spread the butter evenly. While the processor is running, drop the egg into the bowl and stop the machine as soon as the frangipane comes together and the egg is evenly distributed. Transfer into a bowl and set aside. You can wrap the frangipane tightly in plastic wrap and keep it in the fridge for a few days or in the freezer for a few weeks.

Frangipane fruit tart

SERVES 6 to 8

1 pâte sablée recipe (page 116)
1 frangipane recipe (page 125)
3 to 4 large peaches, or 10 to 12 apricots, or both

EQUIPMENT: *9-inch* | *23-cm tart pan*
PREHEAT THE OVEN TO: *375°F* | *190°C* | *Gas Mark 5*

Line the tart pan with the pâte sablée. Fill the tart with the frangipane about two-thirds of the way to the top. Put any remaining frangipane back in the fridge immediately.

Cut each peach into 6 to 8 wedges, depending on the size. If using the apricots, cut them in half and place each one, cut-side up, around the pan. Arrange the peach wedges in a tight circle, pressing them slightly into the frangipane cream.

Place the tart pan on the lower shelf of the oven with a baking sheet on the bottom to catch any spills. Bake for 45 minutes, or until the tart crust is golden and the frangipane is cooked through or until slightly springy and brown on top.

Tomato tart with Parmesan crust

I had this tomato tart for the first time at the famous La Régalade in Paris. It offers a perfect contrast between the buttery, savory crust and the bright freshness of the tomatoes. Alas, La Régalade was long shuttered and the chef, Yves Camdeborde, moved on to his new venture by the carrefour de l'Odéon called, simply, Le Comptoir. The tomato tart, as far as I could tell, didn't make it to the new location, so I had to re-create the dish on my own. It can be served as the first course of a multicourse dinner, or paired with a simple

green salad for a satisfying lunch. This recipe is based loosely on the recipe published by the chef in his cookbook *La Régalade*.

SERVES 4 AS PART OF A MAIN COURSE, OR 6 AS A STARTER

PASTRY CRUST
1¹/2 cups | 200g plain flour
³/4 cup | 100g freshly grated Parmesan cheese
1¹/2 cups | 200g plus 1 tablespoon unsalted butter, cold but soft, close to
*   room temperature*

TOMATO FILLING
3 to 4 large heirloom tomatoes or 8 to 10 small tomatoes
¹/2 tablespoon kosher salt or fleur de sel
a few chunks of mozzarella (optional)

EQUIPMENT: *Food processor, a 10-inch/25-cm fluted tart pan with a*
*   removable bottom, pie weights (you can use raw rice, dried beans,*
*   or even a big pile of pennies for this)*
PREHEAT THE OVEN TO: *375°F | 190°C | Gas Mark 5*

First prepare the crust. In the bowl of a food processor, add all three ingredients and hit pulse repeatedly about 5 to 10 times. The ingredients will begin to mix together and turn a little bit sandy. When the dough resembles clumpy wet sand, process it for about 7 to 10 seconds, just until the dough forms a ball. Empty the processor bowl onto a wooden board. Knead the dough gently a few times by picking up one corner and folding the dough over itself and pressing it down lightly with the palm of your hand. Repeat this four or five times. Use a dough scraper to pick up any stray bits and fold them into the middle, folding the dough over itself and pressing down with your palm. At this point the dough should be the consistency of Play-doh modeling clay and very easy to work.

Lining the pan: The press method
At this stage, the dough can be pressed immediately into a 10-inch/25-cm tart pan but make sure your hands are cold while doing this or everything will turn into a sticky mess. (I occasionally find it helpful

to use a sheet of plastic wrap between my hand and the tart dough.) Take the dough in your hands and press it evenly against the bottom and up the sides of the pan. Wrap the lined tart pan with plastic wrap and let it rest in the fridge for 30 minutes to 1 hour before use. If you wrap it tightly you can keep the prepared shell until the next day, which is quite handy to do ahead for a party. Or, you can simply leave the dough at the resting stage for 30 minutes or overnight. In this case, press the dough into a 4- to 5-inch/10- to 12-cm disc, wrap it tightly with plastic wrap and let it rest in the refrigerator until you are ready to use it.

Lining the pan: The roll method

If you prefer to roll the dough instead of pressing it directly into the pan (I find rolling easier myself) you should let the dough rest for about an hour or up to a day in the fridge. To pack the dough for resting, roll it into a large ball and flatten it slightly into 5- to 6-inch/12- to 15-cm wide and about a bit over 1-inch/2-cm deep disc and wrap it tightly in plastic wrap. Reserve it in the fridge until you are ready to use it. You can even freeze this for use later. (It will keep in the freezer for 3 months. Just thaw it overnight in the fridge the day before you need to use it.)

When you are ready to roll, take the dough out of the fridge. If the dough has been there over an hour, let it temper out of the fridge for a while before rolling or pressing it into the tart pan. It should be pliable and roll without breaking. Roll the dough into a circle large enough for the pan. The rolled-out dough should be about $1^{1}/_{2}$- to 2-inch/3.5- to 5-cm wider than the rim of the tart pan, all around.

Now press the dough into the pan. Pick up the overhanging dough and push it down into the bottom corner and the side of the tart shell. Press it firmly to set the dough against the pan. This way your shell will be the same thickness all around, and will bake evenly. Prick the bottom of the tart with the tines of a fork, being careful not to puncture the shell all the way through. Just pricking the surface allows some air to escape and prevents the bottom of the tart from buckling up during the pre-baking.

Cut a piece of parchment paper or foil quite a bit larger than the diameter of the tart pan. Put it over on top of the lined pan and fill the top with pie weights. Place the shell in the oven for 20 minutes.

While the dough is baking, you can prepare the tomatoes. Line a large baking tray with paper towels. Wash and dry the tomatoes and slice them into about $1/2$-inch/1-cm slices. Lay them down side by side on the baking sheet, and don't allow them to overlap. Sprinkle the salt or fleur de sel over the slices and let the juice drain out for about 20 minutes.

After the shell has been in the oven for 20 minutes, remove it to cool for a few minutes, and turn the oven up to 400°F/200°C/Gas Mark 6. When the pastry shell is cool enough to touch without burning yourself, you're ready to line it with the tomato slices and finish the tart.

Take another length of paper towels and press it gently over the top of the tomato slices to remove any excess liquid. Gently pick up each slice of tomato and line the tart with them, overlapping slightly, until the tart is completely covered. Return the tart to the oven and bake for another 15 minutes or just until the tart crust is beautifully golden. If you want to be even more indulgent, break up a few chunks of fresh mozzarella, and scatter them all over the tart about 10 minutes before it finishes baking. Remove the tart from the oven and let it stand for 5 to 10 minutes before cutting it into slices and serving.

Foodie ideas

You can also use this dough recipe to bake up the most delectable Parmesan sablée savory biscuits. These sablées will be so delicate they practically crumble at the mere sight. To make the sablées, roll the dough into a log, wrap with plastic wrap or parchment paper and refrigerate for at least an hour. Then cut them into $1/4$-inch/5-mm rounds, and bake at 375°F/190°C/Gas Mark 5 for 15 to 18 minutes or until golden brown. Serve them with cheese or as an hors-d'oeuvre.

Tarte sablée au chocolat

Adapted from Bernard Pacaud of L'Ambroisie, Paris

L'Ambroisie, the venerable Paris restaurant at Place des Vosges, has been a long-time favorite of mine. This delicate chocolate tart, distinguished from other chocolate tarts in the universe by its light-as-air whipped chocolate filling, is my lovely way to end every meal at that restaurant.

PÂTE SABLÉE

2/3 cup | 150g butter, room temperature
2/3 teaspoon salt
1/3 cup | 75g sugar
1 egg
1 1/2 cups | 200g flour

CHOCOLATE FILLING

10oz | 300g plain chocolate
2 eggs
4 egg yolks
1/4 cup | 60g sugar
3/4 cup | 200g butter, at room temperature

EQUIPMENT: *12-inch | 30-cm fluted tart pan with a removable base, pie weights (you can use raw rice, dried beans, or even a big pile of pennies for this)*

TO SERVE: *Vanilla ice cream or whipped cream*

PREHEAT THE OVEN TO: *350°F | 180°C | Gas Mark 4*

Add the butter, salt, sugar, and egg to the bowl of a food processor and process until the mixture is well blended. Add the flour and pulse a few times just until the flour and butter mixture are well incorporated. The texture will look like clumpy wet sand. Pulse a few more times until it all comes together to form dough.

From this point you can do one of two things. Either press the dough into a tart pan right away, or let the dough rest before rolling it out to fill the tart pan. I think it's just as easy either way. Some people seem to be afraid of the rolling, in which case pressing the dough right into the tart pan with your fingers would be an easier choice.

To press the dough into the tart pan, wrap a piece of plastic wrap around one hand and use that wrapped hand to press the dough into the shell. Take care to spread it evenly on the tart pan. To work on the side of the pan, wrap one finger of your other hand with a piece of plastic wrap. Press this finger down at the top of the rim of the pan, levelling the dough at the rim as your other hand presses the dough into the side of the pan. This will create an even wall around the tart shell.

To finish, tear off a length of plastic wrap large enough to cover the entire surface of the pastry-lined tart pan. Press the plastic wrap into the bottom of the tart and against the side wall. Press down slightly on any uneven patches to flatten the dough and make the pastry shell level all over. Wrap the pan with plastic wrap and let it rest in the fridge for 2 hours or overnight, before use.

If you are planning to roll the pastry shell, once the dough gathers into a ball, press it down to a 4-inch/10-cm disc, wrap it in clingflim and let it rest for at least 2 hours (or overnight) in the fridge. After the dough has rested, roll it out into a 13-inch/33-cm circle on a lightly floured, impeccably clean work surface. Pick up one side of the rolled-out dough and carefully wrap it loosely over the rolling pin. Slip it gently off of the rolling pin and into the tart pan. Pick up the edge of the dough and push in and down into the side of the pan. This will ensure an even layer at the edge of the pan and keep the dough from shrinking too much during baking. Don't worry if the dough is broken in parts. Just press the dough back together, or patch any crack with excess dough. Once the dough is in place, take your rolling pin and roll it quickly over the top of the tart. The excess dough should fall away from the rim easily, leaving clean, even edges on the lined tart pan.

Cut a piece of aluminum foil or parchment paper larger than the diameter of the tart, place it on top of the tart and fill the top with pie weights. Distribute the weights all over the surface of the pastry shell, and right into the side walls. This prevents the tart from puffing up and shrinking too much during pre-baking (or blind baking, as they say in baking circles). Bake the tart shell for 12 minutes. Remove the tart from the oven. Remove the pie weights and discard the foil. Let the shell cool while you prepare the chocolate filling.

Break the chocolate into chunks and place it in a *bain marie*, which is just a fancy way of saying a large bowl over a pot of gently simmering water, making sure the water doesn't touch the bowl. When the chocolate has melted, set the bowl aside to cool. Beat the eggs, the yolks, and the sugar in another bowl until they pale. The goal here is to get to what's called the ribbon stage. This means that when you pick up your whisk, flick your wrist a little, and let the mixture fall off into a bowl it creates a nice ribbon-ish form on the surface. Whisk the butter into the cooled chocolate and pour the mixture into the eggs and sugar. Continue to whisk until everything is well incorporated. Then pour the mixture into the cool part-baked tart.

Place the tart in the oven and bake it for 18 to 20 minutes. When it comes out of the oven let it stand until it is just slightly warm.

Serve it plain, with vanilla ice cream, or with a dollop of whipped cream for extra indulgence. At L'Ambroisie, the consummate host Pierre Lemoullac – Monsieur Pierre as everyone affectionately calls him – insists on serving it with beautifully aged Scotch. Try as I might, I never could resist him.

Brilliant au Caramel

Recipe adapted from Pierre and Michel Troisgros

This chocolate caramel tart is Pierre and Michel Troisgros' signature dessert and has been a firm favourite with diners and a fixture on the menu at Maison Troisgros for decades.

SERVES 6 to 8

1 recipe pâte sablée (page 116)

CHOCOLATE GANACHE
3¹/₂oz | 100g dark chocolate (at least 70% cocoa solids)
¹/₂ cup | 120ml heavy cream

CARAMEL
5¹/₂oz | 160g sugar
5 tablespoons | 80g salted butter, room temperature
3 tablespoons water
¹/₂ cup plus 2 tablespoons heavy cream
1¹/₂ teaspoons lemon juice

EQUIPMENT: *9-inch | 23-cm tart pan with a removable base, quick-read thermometer (optional), piping bag with a star or round nozzle (or a self-sealing plastic bag)*
PREHEAT THE OVEN TO: *350°F | 180°C | Gas Mark 4*

Prepare the tart shell first by lining a 9-inch/23-cm tart pan with pâte sablée (following methods on page 130) and bake until done. Transfer to a rack to cool completely.

While the tart is cooling, chop up the chocolate. Add the cream to a medium-sized saucepan and place over low heat and bring to a gently

HOW TO COOK LIKE A FOODIE

simmer. Add the chopped chocolates to the pan and let sit for 2 minutes to melt. Whisk until the ganache is smooth and let rest until it has cooled down a bit.

Transfer the chocolate ganache to a piping bag with a medium round nozzle (or a fancy star tip if you're in the mood). Pipe the ganache to form a border around the edge of the tart, then four crisscrossing lines to form the outline of eight pie wedges. Put the tart in the fridge to cool until it has firmly set.

While waiting for the ganache to set you can make the caramel. In a medium pan, add the sugar and let it dissolve gently over medium heat. Shake the pan occasionally to make sure all the sugar has dissolved. Stir if you need to. Add the cream to another small pan and bring to a gentle simmer. When the sugar dissolves and turns amber, add the cream to it and stir vigorously to mix well. Add the butter in small chunks and stir to blend. Set the caramel aside to cool down until lukewarm but still liquid.

Spoon the cooled caramel into each of the outlined sections of the chilled tart. When ready to serve, cut along the ganache border so the caramel doesn't gush out.

You can also use this recipe to make smaller, individual tarts. Instead of making the full recipe in a large pan, use six or eight smaller ones. You won't need to pipe ganache borders for the small tarts, just divide the caramel evenly between the baked tart shells, let cool to set (for at least an hour), then spoon the ganache over the layer of caramel. The caramel will ooze out as you take a bite.

Gooey chocolate cake baked in a jar

This is a cute and meltingly delicious chocolate "cake" recipe, baked right into jam jars or even small, heat-proof drinking glasses or cups and will add a little whimsy to the end of your meal. You can divide this batter in six or eight portions, depending on the containers you have on hand – they don't even need to match. I should tell you that this is a very rich dessert, so even a small portion goes a long way.

Continued

¹/₃ cup | 100g butter
5oz | 150g good-quality plain chocolate
1 egg
2 yolks
³/₄oz | 20g sugar

EQUIPMENT: *6 to 8 jam jars or small heat-proof drinking glasses or cups*
TO SERVE: *Whipped cream flavored with vanilla or vanilla extract*
PREHEAT THE OVEN TO: *325°F | 160°C | Gas Mark 3.*

Add the butter to a small saucepan set over medium heat. Melt the butter down completely, then let simmer over very low heat until you are ready to use it. The butter must be kept very hot.

Place the chocolate in a double boiler or a medium-sized bowl set over a pot of simmering water (for full instructions on melting chocolate, see page 134). Once it has melted, set it aside.

Place the whole egg, yolks, and sugar in a large bowl and whip them together until they are light in color. This process does not take much effort and is easily done by hand.

In another large bowl, add the melted chocolate and the hot melted butter, and whisk them vigorously until they are well combined. Add this mixture into the egg and sugar mixture, and whisk quickly until just combined. Divide this batter equally between six to eight jars.

Fill a brownie pan up to 2 inches/5cm deep with water, and arrange the chocolate-filled jars evenly in two rows in the tin. Bake for 5 to 7 minutes or until the cakes are cooked on the side but still loose in the center. Remove them from the oven and leave them to cool. Serve with whipped cream.

Foodie ideas
Hide a delicious dried *pruneaux d'Agen* (or other type of prune you can get your hands on) at the bottom of the jar before filling with chocolate, and serve the dessert with aged Armagnac. You can also hide candied orange peel or other candied fruits in the jar before adding the chocolate batter, and perhaps serve the finished dessert with Grande Marnier.

Alfajores

Your life as a foodie is not complete until you've tried *alfajores* (pronounced al-fah-ho-res), two buttery, crumbly cookies hugging sweet dulce de leche (milk confection). *Alfajores* are found all over Latin America, each country claiming an authentic recipe of its own. This particular *alfajores* recipe is adapted from one in the Argentine style. Once baked, the cookies are so delicate they seem to crumble under too intense a gaze. But while they are being made, the dough is so easy to work with it feels like modeling clay. Make these little heavenly cookies for your next party. You might have to spend half the night teaching your friends how to say *alfajores*, but they will adore you for it.

MAKES APPROXIMATELY 30 SANDWICH COOKIES

2 cups | 250g cornstarch (sifted method)
1¹/2 cups | 200g plain flour
¹/2 teaspoon salt
2 teaspoons baking powder
¹/2 teaspoon baking soda
³/4 cup | 200g butter at room temperature
¹/3 cup | 75g sugar
3 egg yolks
1 tablespoon Cognac
1 cup dulce de leche (page 140)

TO SERVE: *Confectioners' sugar for sifting, coconut flakes*
EQUIPMENT: *3-inch | 6- to 7-cm fluted pastry cutter, stand mixer, piping bag with a large nozzle*

If you don't have kitchen scales, this recipe should be enough for you to go get one. Cornstarch is notoriously difficult to measure in volume, but if you don't have a kitchen scale and don't want to buy one, you can sift the cornstarch directly to a measuring cup. Line your work surface with a large piece of parchment paper. Place a one-cup dry measure in the middle of it. Pour the cornstarch into a sieve or a large strainer and sift it directly over the measuring cup. Continue sifting until you fill the cup with sifted cornstarch. You can tap the cup just to let the cornstarch

settle, but do it very gently as you don't want to pack cornstarch tightly into it. Level the top with the back of a knife. When you're done measuring, gather the paper and pour the excess cornstarch back into the box. Measuring this way you should get about 250g from two cups, precisely what you need in this recipe

Preheat the oven to 350°F/175°C/Gas Mark 4. Sift the flour, cornstarch, salt, baking powder and baking soda together in a bowl and set it aside.

In the bowl of a stand mixer, beat the butter, sugar, and egg yolks on high speed until they are well incorporated. Then add the Cognac and beat until combined. Reduce the speed to low, and add the dry ingredients a bit at a time until they are well incorporated. Empty the bowl onto a dry board and knead the mixture just until it comes together into dough. Divide the dough into two balls. At this point you can wrap each ball with plastic wrap and store them in the fridge for up to a day until you're ready to use them.

If the dough has been refrigerated, let it sit out at room temperature for a short time to warm up a bit. Then, on a lightly floured work surface, roll each ball of dough out until it is ¼ inch/5mm thick. Use a 3-inch/6- to 7-cm fluted pastry cutter to cut 20 to 25 cookies from each half of the dough. You can gather the excess dough together and roll it again. (This dough is very forgiving.) Place the cut cookies onto two large baking sheets, leaving just ½ inch/1cm between them – they only expand a tiny bit while baking.

Bake for 15 to 20 minutes, switching the baking sheets about halfway through. The cookies should change color only slightly. Remove them from the oven immediately. Let then stand on the baking sheet for about 2 minutes. Then, handling them gently, transfer them onto a rack to cool.

To finish the cookies, fill a piping bag with the dulce de leche. Pipe about 1 tablespoon on the top of half of the cookies. If you don't have a piping bag, just spread the dulce de leche onto the cookies using a palette knife but be careful because these cookies are very delicate. Top the filled cookies with the remaining cookies, to make cookie sandwiches, pressing down a little so the filling spreads evenly. Sift a bit of confectioners' sugar on top just before serving. You can also roll the side of the cookies over coconut flakes to make them even more delicious (and authentic).

Dulce de leche

If you can't find a jar of dulce de leche, you can easily make your own.

14fl oz | 400g can of condensed milk
1 vanilla pod

PREHEAT THE OVEN TO: *425°F | 220°C | Gas Mark 7*

Open the can of condensed milk and pour it into a medium-sized baking pan. (I use a glass Pyrex pie dish for this.) Cut the vanilla pod in half lengthwise and scrape out the seeds. Add them to the condensed milk and mix well. You can even throw in the pod as well, and just remove it after the cooking. Cover the baking pan with aluminum foil.

Place the baking pan in a larger pan with high sides. Add water to the larger pan until it comes halfway up the side of the small pan. Place it in the oven and bake for about an hour. Check it every so often to make sure there's still water in the pan, and refill it as necessary.

Remove the pan from the oven, and take out the vanilla pod. Whisk the mixture until the texture is smooth. Let it cool to room temperature before using.

Lychee and orange *loy gaew*

Loy gaew is a very common way of serving fresh tropical fruits as a dessert course in Thailand, and the name literally means "floating crystals," referring to the crushed ice floating in clear syrup in this recipe. Just about any fruit could be cut up and added to this slightly salty syrup. This version is my adaptation of an old recipe called *Som Chun*, which originally calls for tart, fresh lychees and a few other things that may not be easy to find.

You should prepare the *loy gaew* before you cook your meal, in order to give the mixture a little bit of macerating time in the fridge before serving.

SERVES 8

SYRUP
3 cups | 750g sugar
4 cups | 950ml water
5-inch | 12-cm piece of ginger, peeled and thinly sliced
1 to 2 teaspoons salt

LOY GAEW
^{1}/4 cup | 20g tightly packed shredded coconut
6 medium-sized oranges
Two 20oz | 575g cans lychees, drained, or 2^1/2 cups | 475g fresh lychees,
    peeled and seeded
handful of fresh mint

TO SERVE: *Crushed ice*

Make the syrup by mixing the sugar, water, ginger slices, and salt in a
medium-sized pot. Bring to a boil, then reduce the heat to a simmer and
continue to cook for 20 minutes or until the liquid is reduced by almost
half. Set aside to cool.

  Place a frying pan over medium-low heat. Add the coconut and
toss it around until the flakes turn golden brown. Make sure you stir
or toss the coconut frequently or it will burn before it browns evenly.
When it has finished browning, spread the coconut flakes out on a plate
to cool. Set aside.

  Peel and segment the oranges and place them in a large bowl.
Add the lychees and set aside. When the syrup is completely cool,
remove the ginger slices with a slotted spoon and discard. Then pour
the syrup into the bowl with the oranges and lychees. Throw in the
handful of fresh mint, cover the bowl with plastic wrap and place in
the fridge to chill.

  Serve as a dessert soup with plenty of crushed ice. Sprinkle the
toasted coconut flakes over each serving at the very last minute.

3 | How to drink like a foodie

How not to be a wine geek

Yes, you read the title right. It says how *not* to be a wine geek. This is not a *How To* guide, so much as a *How Not To* guide. What's a wine geek, you asked? I'm sure you've met some of them, for they are legion. Wine geeks remember the Parker score of every current-release Bordeaux, Burgundy, and/or cult California cab, probably with at least some Super Tuscan thrown in too, as well as Margaret River Cab and Shiraz. They probably even have a Parker vintage report loaded on their laptop. They buy wine based on expert scores posted ever so conveniently right by the wine bins in the store. The value of a wine is, according to them, based on an unknown or, at best, barely understood criteria set forth by someone else. They taste wine in earnest, identifying whiffs of impossible minutiae, a soupçon of this flower or that spice or the seventeen other scents in the glass. In short, they are no fun to be around.

Fortunately, you need not succumb to wine-geekdom to appreciate wine. We don't all have to turn into human spreadsheets, remembering every single score by every single influential critic. I don't understand why people pay so much attention to wine scores anyway, especially the 100-point scoring system made popular by Robert Parker, the emperor of wine himself. It's ludicrous when you really think about it. First of all, have you ever seen a wine that scores less than 50 points? I sure haven't. It's as though the simple act of bottling a purple liquid with a bit of alcohol entitles the wineries to half the total score already.

Doesn't make much sense, does it?

Mind you, I don't suggest we all sink to the boxed wine level. I have a sneaking suspicion that people who drink that stuff don't like wine or even want to drink wine. Such wines are not horrid, mind you, but they are crafted not to taste much of anything, and take the path of least resistance so as to offend the fewest consumers. The result is wine that is so flavorless, flat, and uninteresting that they hardly taste like wine anymore. I'm not entirely sure why people drink it. If all they want to do is get drunk they can do it much more efficiently with a bottle of Russian vodka.

However, scoring all wines against a single set of all-encompassing criteria is too reductionist an approach to work well for our enjoyment of wine. The biggest thing this approach left out was how contextual a wine experience could be. The best wine to drink on a hot summer afternoon and the one to drink with a hearty *coq au vin* in front of a raging fire on a cold, damp winter night are clearly not the same. What works brilliantly in one situation most likely fails miserably in the other. So, who cares if one scores 95 while the other 87?

The manner in which many wines are scored also makes me skeptical of the system. Experts who go to trade tasting sessions or conduct tastings with multiple wines do the swirl, sniff, sip, and spit method (or some variation thereof). How could they possibly judge a wine in that way? Wines are made for drinking, not spitting out!

I'm hardly the only one who mistrusts the scoring system. Joe Dressner writes a fantastically idiosyncratic blog entitled "A Wine Importer Thinking Out Loud," which I follow rather religiously. He has been arguing that point for years. An importer himself, he steadfastly refuses to play the system, preferring to describe his wines rather than assigning a number or noting scores from "experts."

So, if we don't follow the experts' scores posted on the bins at Trader Joe's or Whole Foods, what are we to do? Well, I follow Joe Dressner's advice. A bottle of wine is to be consumed and appreciated in its context. That means not only in the moment and in partner with the food being served, but also as a cultural artifact. A bottle of wine is not merely a commodity to be reduced to a set of descriptors or characteristics or assigned a number, but a link on a chain rich in culture and *his*tory (and *her*story). It was made in a particular place and came with all the stories about the people and the practice that went into the making of that wine. Learning about those stories and those people helps me understand the wine and appreciate my experience drinking it.

You could say that my own approach to learning about wine is far from the statistical: learning the value of the individual bottles of wine and their associated scores is like chasing a mirage in a desert. You can almost see it shimmering just over there, but you'll never make it, no matter how fast you run. I prefer to grow my knowledge more organically.

Make friends with a retailer A really good way to learn about wine is to find a good wine shop near you and become a regular customer. The shop must stock good wines and have at least one knowledgeable member of staff with whom you could have a conversation about wine. The goal is to have someone understand your palate and preference well enough to help you choose the wines you should try in their shop. To have this happen you must frequent the shop, making it economically viable for them to invest in knowing your preferences and predilections. You must also give feedback, letting them know how you like or dislike the wines they recommend.

Trust producers or importers I believe in placing my trust not on the bottles or the value assigned to them by those who do the 20-second tasting but in the people behind the wines. In other words, I rely on the producers who made the wines and the importers who bring them to me (in the case of foreign wines).

When I wanted to seriously learn about wine, I asked my friend the wine writer Claude Kolm for advice on how to choose good wine. He said straight away that the easiest thing to do was to turn the bottle around and read the name of the importer. Good importers care deeply about their reputation and have strong styles that we can both identify and identify with, and will only bring in good wines that they can put their name behind.

In the same vein, good producers have all of those qualities. That doesn't mean that we should all be blinded by the grand reputation of fancy domaines and châteaux. Learning about the history of great producers, how they came to be where they are now and what they are doing to control quality and remain at the top is just as much fun as learning about young, up-and-coming producers who are fighting an uphill battle to establish their reputation and produce high-quality products.

I don't believe you can judge wine in the bottle as if it had been produced in a vacuum. Wine is a natural product, a delicious result of an ecosystem that affects the natural environment. It comes from the land, with each flavor and scent representing the characteristics of where and what it originated from. Understanding all of this helps me better appreciate the wine in my glass. It also helps me choose the next glass or the next bottle, by following the products of the same producers or those with similar intentions and practices.

Finding your favourite appellations and producers can give you the language of wine you need to communicate with the professionals. When faced with an unfamiliar wine list without a name you recognize, instead of trying for the "seventeen spices and five blossoms" you want in your bottle for that particular dinner, you can simply say, I'd like a lighter, more delicate Burgundy, something like a Chambolle Musigny from Fréderic Mugnier.

Trust good sommeliers   When I am at a restaurant and feel particularly good about my rapport with the sommelier, I often ask her or him to introduce me to a wine I may not have thought of ordering on my own. I've learned so much this way, and have been introduced to many wines that I wouldn't have found by myself. Some of my all-time favorite wines were introduced to me by great and generous sommeliers from my best-loved restaurants. My two favorite Saumurs (Château Yvonne and Clos de Rougeard), in particular, were wines I wouldn't have encountered on my own but for the introduction in a pairing by Christophe Rohat at L'Astrance in Paris.

Delve into a wine region or varietal   When learning about new wines, my preferred method is to pick a region (or, less often, a varietal) and find out as much as I can about it. I find out about the grapes grown in that region, the style of wine made there, and familiarize myself with a number of reputable producers in the area. Spending the time to learn about a region will teach you not only the prevalent style there but also nuanced differences within the region, say, Northern or Southern Rhône, for example. Okay, that's not exactly

nuanced, but I didn't want to scare you by saying the difference between Chambolle Musigny and Gevrey Chambertin in Burgundy.

Learn recent vintage variations   I'm not asking you to memorize the vintage charts that date back to the beginning of the last century, but being aware of a few of the recent vintage characteristics of some of your favorite wine regions could be helpful. For example, just knowing that 2003 was a very hot and tough year for Burgundy can help you either avoid seemingly good deals on wine lists or find an overlooked bargain.

Know the critics   Don't think that I don't listen to any of the critics at all. I do. However, what I pay attention to is the narrative about the wine and its quality, not the score they assign. Numbers alone don't mean much. Someone else's 96 can easily be my 56. The only way to know what a score of 86 from one critic means is by understanding the subjective preferences of the critic himself (or herself). Find a critic whose taste you can identify with, and who likes the same wines that you do. Use their reviews and advice as guidelines. They taste a lot more wines than you do so their opinions can be useful. Just don't follow them blindly, lest you go "b-a-h" like a sheep.

Learn some of the lexicons of wines   Our human brain is wired to pick up patterns and differences, so if you want to learn what an oaky wine tastes like, taste two wines side by side. For example, try two Chardonnay-based white wines, such as a bottle of French Chablis and a California Chardonnay (ask your wine merchant to select a really oaky producer). Taste the two wines side by side, and you will immediately know what oaky means in the wine lexicon. Comparing those two specific wines will also teach you the differences in the body and structure.

Take useful notes   Don't be long-winded about your tasting notes. I don't really see much value in identifying all the seventeen different things in the nose and palate of a wine. Writing down "a soupçon of this and that…" is more annoying than helpful. Instead, take notes that will be useful to you in the future. How did you like the wine? How did it taste? What was the body or structure of the wine like? Was it light or thick and viscous? Was it fruity or earthy? What other characteristics were obvious to you? What food did you have with it? How was the pairing? Was it successful? Would you serve that food again with that wine? If not, what was the problem? What was missing in the food or the wine that kept them from being a perfect match? When did you drink the wine? Was the timing appropriate? If not, when would be a better time? Answering these questions in your notes will help you understand what the wine was in context and how to drink or serve it in the future, which is far better than listing all the minutiae of spices in the "nose."

Pairing food and wine

Food and wine pairing is not a matter of memorizing a large database of what food goes with which wine, and having the ability to instantaneously recall any one of those rigid matches. The real key to pairing is to understand the effect and the rapport that food and wine have on each other when matched on the dinner (or lunch) table.

There are no rules. Well, perhaps there are a few, but most of them more resemble guidelines than they do specific rules. Think about it. Unless you are having a long gastronomic tasting menu at a fancy restaurant, where each course and each bite is specifically matched to a particular wine, you'll most likely want a bottle of white and a bottle of red for dinner, perhaps with a bottle of bubbly to start if you're being indulgent about it. Those few bottles should be versatile enough to last you through dinner and be a reasonable match with the food you serve.

Here are some things I do, and do not do, when pairing food with wine.

Do...
Match the texture of the food and the wine. A fish dish with creamy sauce should be matched with a white wine with a little bit more body, such as white Burgundy.
Match bright, acidic dishes with light, floral white.
Match slightly sweet wine with spicy-hot dishes. Sugar helps lessen the effect of chile on the palate.

Match spicy dishes with big, spicy, juicy red wine. For this I'm only talking about dishes that are spice-spicy and not chile-spicy. In this case, spices in the wine and spices in the food will complement each other instead of clash, as would spicy wine with a chile-hot dish.

Match big, tannic red wines with fatty food. For thousands of years the Chinese have paired tannic oolong teas with fatty dishes like roast Peking duck or five-spice braised pork belly. Matching wine with these fatty foods follows the same logic. Tannin in wine helps cut through the fat and refresh the palate fatigued with oily food.

Match earthy wine with earthy food. Earthy flavors like mushrooms or truffles, meat braised in red wine, or chicken that has been cooked for a long time are all great matches with earthy wine like Burgundy or Northern Rhône wines.

Match food and wine that have both developed in the same region. The old adage of drinking local wine with local food works especially well in regions that have a long tradition of developing food and wine. It's hard to argue with years of trial and error. On the other hand, big, juicy California Cabernet Sauvignon is not exactly a great match with the region's market-driven, seasonal approach to cooking.

Match bubbly wines or Champagnes to just about anything. Enough said.

Don't…

Match austere, acidic wine with savory dishes with sweet overtones. The sweetness in the food will cause the wine to taste even more acidic and harsh. Pair acidic dishes with slightly off-dry or sweet wine to keep the acidity of the wine in check.

Serve tannic red wine with spicy-hot dishes. Tannin will turn the dish acrid, so serve juicy red wine instead. The slight sugar in the wine will mitigate the effect of the heat.

Serve high-alcohol wine with spicy (chile-hot) dishes. Alcohol exacerbates the effect of chile, and will make the dish even more harsh and spicy.

Follow the old adage: red meat with red wine, white meat with white wine. That's so old-fashioned it stopped being useful at least fifteen years ago. What matters more is the dish rather than the protein. How the meat or fish are prepared and how will they be served will affect the choice of wine.

Wine and Thai food, a marriage destined for failure?

I cook a lot of Thai food, and I love wine, so I am often asked my opinion about serving wine with Thai food. With rampant spices, at times out-of-control heat, bitter herbs, cloying sweetness, sometimes all of those qualities in one dish, Thai food (or other Southeast Asian food) can be a rather tough match with wine. It also doesn't help much that over in Asia, one of the biggest selling wines is Bordeaux, which is hardly a match with the food by any criteria.

Johannes Selbach, the winemaker and proprietor of Domaine Selbach-Oster in Germany, and I had a good conversation about this once. He wondered why the Riesling market in Asia is so small, when the wine is such a perfect match for the food. "People are drinking fancy Bordeaux and cult Australian Shiraz!" he exclaimed, clearly surprised. I have my own theory about this. I think people in Asia care a little less about this because they are not as bothered by the effect of food and wine clashing. Big and tannic Bordeaux get even bigger and more tannic with Asian dishes, turning bitter and acrid when pairing with the spices and heat in the food. Bitter flavor is not alien to that cuisine, however, and can even be desirable. There is a Chinese term, *gan*, which explains a sort of desirable bitterness that could be translated as bittersweet, but it isn't really. It's just a different kind of bitterness that one finds in prized food, such as ginseng and exquisite teas.

So, unless you are of Asian descent and have a special fondness of *gan* food, here are a few keys I use in matching wine with Thai food. The same practice applies to other Southeast Asian cuisines as well. These are not rules, mind you. I hardly believe in rigid rules about anything (well, unless I'm the one making them). These are merely suggestions. Experiment with them and see what works for you. Wine and food are for fun, after all, so enjoy yourself!

Look for a little sweetness and the tropics It has become almost a reflex for me to reach for a bottle of slightly sweet Riesling when serving Thai food, and with very good reason. The slight sweetness and floral notes in Rieslings and similar wines (like Gewürztraminer) match very well with the many flavors of Thai food. The sugar adds to the mouth-feel of wine and mitigates the effect of chile and spice on the palate. Sweetness in wine also works well with the savory dishes that are on the sweet side in Thai cuisine. Try and find the tropics in the nose, too. Well, not your nose, but the nose of a wine. Some wines smell of tropical flowers or exotic fruits, which, predictably enough, will match well with the same notes in Thai dishes.

Avoid tannin at all cost   Never drink tannic wines with Thai food. (This one probably most resembles a rule.) The prominent flavors of Thai food (spicy, hot, and sour) are all horrible with big, tannic wines. Spice, chile heat, and acidity will make tannic wine taste bitter, ruining the experience of both the food and the wine. So, keep your fancy Bordeaux and expensive Cabs away from Thai food.

A little sparkly is good for the soul   Sparkling wine works well with Thai food, especially with the many fried dishes in Thai cuisine. The bubbles cut through the fat and refresh the palate. Slightly off-dry Champagne or sparkling wine can also be versatile for many types of Thai dishes. It even works well with a creamy curry, as long as it's not a superspicy one. So, if you're thinking about just one bottle of wine (besides a Riesling) to match the entire Thai meal, pick a bottle of floral Champagne. It will surprise you.

Balanced acidity is key   Thai food has a strong acidic element, especially yum-type salads or the sour curries like *gang som*, which are often dominated by the juice of limes or tamarind. For these types of dishes, it's important that the wine you choose has a good level of acidity to support the acid in the food. Flat, flabby, low-acidity wine will be overwhelmed and turn even flabbier and less acidic when paired with these sour dishes. Acidic wines are also good with salty food, so they pair well with salty Thai dishes. It may sound a little counterintuitive, but even when you choose slightly sweet, off-dry wines, make sure that they have a good level of acidity supporting in the background. Acidity can also be a double-edged sword because very sweet dishes will turn acidic wines even leaner and more acidic, which could be unpleasant. So, if you like your Pad Thai cloyingly sweet, then I would pick slightly sweet wine to go with it.

Leave the oak in the barrel and not in the wine   Oaky wines, like a lot of Californian Chardonnays for example, do not pair well with

Thai food. The predominant vanilla and butter flavors in oaky Chardonnay don't go well with the exotic herbs and spices in Thai food. Stay away from them.

Now that you have some guidelines, here are some wine varietals to go with Thai food. These are just suggestions, covering some of my favorites and include both obvious and more obscure choices. Play around with some of them and see what suits you best.

White:

RIESLING: *and other German/Alsace whites like Gewürztraminer and Pinot Gris.* This is a no-brainer. Go with fruity and floral nose rather than the musky note from the "noble rot" or botrytis evident in some Rieslings.

SCHEUREBE: This wine is a cross between Riesling and Sylvaner. It is crispy, fruity, and very aromatic, and will work well here too.

LOIRE WHITES: *Vouvray, Savennières, and Saumur Blanc.* The crisp minerality and citrus notes in these wines work particularly well with sour Yum salads. Certain Saumur Blanc with good structure (like my favourite Chateau Yvonne) would make a pleasing match for coconut-based dishes, as long as they are not extremely spicy. The minerality in these white wines from the Loire valley also go very well with Thai seafood dishes.

SPARKLING: *Champagne and sparkling rosé.* These wines will work as long as they are not too oaky.

LAMBRUSCO: A sparkling wine from Italy, Lambrusco is fruity and slightly sweet, and will be a fun and unexpected match with Thai food. The French Cerdon de Bugey is quite similar and can work well, too.

Red:

SAUMUR-CHAMPIGNY: Juicy and low-tannin Saumur-Champigny is a good choice if you want red wine.

CRU BEAUJOLAIS: Light and fruity Cru Beaujolais is also quite good.

BARBERA: Made in the very classic style of low tannin, ripe Barbera can be a good match.

This is far, far from a comprehensive list because I'm only talking about the wines I know. Feel free to suggest your own successful matches.

How to choose good value wines from fancy wine lists

I'm going to let you in on my little secret for getting the most value out of sadly depreciating U.S. dollars from *les cartes de vins* at fancy restaurants in Europe. I've been doing this for a while, but never thought to tell anyone about it. You will be the first to know.

It occurred to me that my little trick might be of use to others when, at the beginning of our recent dinner at the lovely Greenhouse in Mayfair, London, a few years back, my friend Tony commented that the sommelier must have taken a liking to me because he spent such a long time concurring with me on which wines to pick for our table. The sommelier on duty that night was a sweet, bespectacled Frenchman who really did spend a lot of time with his nose buried in the list searching for something suitable for us. Something like this happens not infrequently with me, but I'd never really noticed it until Tony made that comment that evening. I had given the sommelier a little puzzle to solve, you see, and he was doing his best to crack it.

It was this: find a bottle of white and a bottle of red for our table to go with the tasting menu we ordered, and not just any bottle of white or red. I didn't want to spend more than £50 to 75 ($75 to 100) per bottle, and I wanted them to be something from lesser-known producers or appellations, local if appropriate. I'm always interested in those wines that can be hard to find back home in America.

You must be wondering if I conjured up this puzzle only to make hapless sommeliers jump through hoops just for my amusement. Even I am not that devious, though there certainly is a method to my apparent lunacy. That price range is where the best deals are to be found in fancy European wine lists, at roughly £50 to 70 or €50 to 100 per bottle (London markup is higher), and I'm not just pulling this number out of thin air. In this price range, the wine directors of these restaurants cannot simply rely on the famous names of first growths or *grands crus*, because even the wholesale prices are far too high to be featured profitably in a wine list at around €100. What they have to do is trust their nose and palate and search for wines from lesser-known appellations or producers, whose prices have not rocketed out of the range of reason.

To me, this is a great test of a good sommelier. Anyone can fill a wine list with fancy Bordeaux, Burgundy, and cult Californian or Australian wines but it takes a good nose and palate to find suitable Jurançon, Anjou, Saumur, Condrieu, or wine from other, lesser-known regions worthy of their company. Even among well-known areas and famous producers, good deals could be found, such as perhaps a white Bordeaux from a *grand cru* producer better known for their reds, or possibly a red Austrian wine instead of their more famous white counterparts.

Often, these sommeliers would proudly show me their secret finds, such as an obscure Saumur producer in Champigny whose red wines can give other more established reds a run for their money, or a deliciously sweet and honey-like Jurançon that's far better than any Sauternes in the same price range.

I also find it far more fun to explore new flavors and try wines that would be difficult for me to find in the United States. Well-known wines from fancy producers I can always find there, often at wholesale prices even. But these secret appellations and small producers are much harder to come by. I have been taken on many delightful journeys, discovering areas, appellations, and producers that were new to me, all by tasting these wines, and simply by asking nicely.

Of course, each person has their own preference when it comes to wine, and sommeliers – great as they may be – cannot read minds. It is

always helpful to tell them your likes and dislikes, so that they can make an educated choice for you. If you are uncomfortable with wine terms and don't feel you could describe your preferences adequately, perhaps you could point out a well-known wine you have previously enjoyed. The more clues you can give, the easier you will make it for a sommelier to help you.

I've used this trick for a while, and have been very happy with the results so far. Try it and let me know what you think. Happy exploring!

Apéritif and digestif: foreplay and a cuddle, culinarily speaking

Foodies who focus only on the meal and the food make the same mistakes as lovers who only think about the sex without realizing the mood-setting power of good foreplay and the enduring impression of a cuddle afterward. Such foodies are missing out on a whole lot. An apéritif sets the stage, tantalizing the taste buds for the meal to come, while great digestifs send guests off in style. It's the art of creating a great first impression and leaving a long lasting one afterward.

I should admit, though, that I came to be a big proponent of serving an apéritif to my guests because my timing as a party hostess is almost always off. My friends might arrive for dinner at eight, but it is often nine, at times much later, before I set out my first course. I learned quickly that providing a great apéritif prevents dinner guests rebelling at having to wait so long for the food and it can even set them in the proper mood.

I can see how people think apéritifs are just a waste of time and money. The sight of a grinning sommelier pushing a cart bearing a giant bucket of ice filled with Champagne bottles, with the necks sticking out in all directions like a menacing sea mine, will scare just about anyone. You can almost see a thought bubble above his head filled with dollar signs, your hard-earned dollars, of course. It's true that Champagnes from those carts are not the best value for your money, and you are better off ordering by the bottle and sharing with the table. Nonetheless, an apéritif is great for setting the stage for the meal. Imagine the bubbles like many, many tiny little fingers massaging your taste buds, awakening and priming them for the many delicious flavors to come.

I draw the line, however, at being pushed cocktails before my meal, which are only there to make the restaurant extra money on your final bill. Raymond Blanc said so himself on his show *Last Restaurant*

Standing. He even turned cocktails into a challenge in one of the episodes. My advice to you is, don't fall for it. Full of harsh alcohol and sometimes a lot of sugar, cocktails will obliterate your palate and zap your appetite. A martini or gimlet before dinner may be hip, but the only occasion that they fit is when you're heading to what's guaranteed to be a horrendous meal, perhaps at a restaurant you know to be bad but a friend enthusiastically recommends, or at a dinner party whose host, while a great friend of yours, is also a phenomenally bad cook. In these cases you would be well advised to drink yourself silly before walking the plank.

There's also another class of apéritif of which I am not a fan, and that is the pastis, vermouth, and the many variations thereof. The French and Italians believe that the herbaceous element of those drinks performs the same awakening function on your taste buds that Champagne bubbles do. Personally, I find the medicinal notes linger a tad too long in my mouth, and interfere with the nuances in the flavors of my meal. If I do serve these drinks as apéritifs at a party I tend to stay on the lighter side. I would offer guests a Lillet Blanc served on the rocks with a slice of orange, instead of the more medicinal Ricard.

What should you look for in an apéritif then? I think bubbles are very good, though I wouldn't serve grand Champagnes that demand a contemplative mood to appreciate them properly. Instead, I like to serve a lighter-bodied Champagne, without a lot of oak. It can be dry (as in Brut) or even a tiny bit off-dry. The French seem to believe that a little sugar gets the appetite going. On the other hand, Harold McGee told me it's the acidity in dry Champagne or white wine that stimulates the appetite, not the sugar.

Well, tell that to Yves Camdeborde (of the dearly departed La Régalade) and his band of merry friends. They set off the bistronimique trend in Paris in the early 1990s and brought into fashion the sparkling Cerdon de Bugey, from eastern France just south of Burgundy. Pink, sweet, and bubbly, the earthy, inexpensive Cerdon served as their declaration of independence from the tyranny of the menacing Champagne carts, just as the food at those gastronomic bistros was a reaction to the more formal, classic fares at Michelin three-star restaurants the bistronomes had fled.

You can even serve a light white wine, well chilled, if you have friends who don't like bubbly, although why you would keep such friends I can't understand. However, in this case I would think of the body and the texture of the wine. Full-bodied, heavier white wines like oaky California Chardonnay won't do very well as an aperitif. With all its buttery vanilla flavor, it will take a few courses over the length of dinner to dissipate completely. I'd go with a lighter Riesling that is not too syrupy instead, or another white with a lighter body.

Sherry also works well as an apéritif. Well, not your grandmother's heavy, super-sweet sherry, but a proper Spanish Jerez. In Spain, I've often been served fino or Manzanilla before a meal. They are delicately light and dry, and really work well especially when paired with their jamón or olives. Along the same lines, once at the restaurant Mugaritz in San Sebastian, I was offered a glass of pineau des Charentes, a white wine that had been fortified with Cognac and aged in oak. It was not a very patriotic move coming from a Spanish sommelier, but I loved it.

If an apéritif is foreplay, titillating your senses and priming them for the feast to come, a digestif is the cuddle afterward that gives you a warm and fuzzy feeling, extending that afterglow of a fantastic . . . er, meal just a little longer. The French believe that a glass of digestif helps digest the food and settle the stomach after a heavy meal, hence the name. (And trust the French to come up with a medicinal reason to drink yet more alcohol.) Also, trust me to play favorites with a French spirit, Armagnac. There are so many spirits served as a digestif – port, Madeira, Pedro Ximénez, brandy, Cognac, to name but a few – but my heart belongs to Armagnac.

Sadly, most Cognac today is mass-produced to meet increasing demand, especially in the growing market in China. The results are not awful but mostly one-dimensional and uninteresting, sort of like a boring but steady boyfriend. Armagnac, on the other hand, can be a temperamental lover, an artist whose moods change on a whim. It's the kind of relationship that can end in tears, but when all goes as planned it's fireworks and a sky full of stars.

Cognac is distilled twice, while Armagnac is distilled only once, and spends more time in oak barrels. While Cognac is blended to create a consistent flavor profile from year to year, Armagnac producers date each vintage because the characteristics of Armagnac vary from year to year. Ardent Armagnac fans believe that the double distillation of Cognac strips them of most of the fascinating characteristics, and that it's in the Armagnac where one can still taste the true *terroir* of Gascony.

I don't know about you, but when I drink a glass of great Armagnac I definitely get Gascony: a little bit of spice, like the *quatres épices* they use so much in that region, with a little coffee perhaps, also a little confit of fruits, and definitely, inescapably, prunes.

The best temperature to drink Armagnac is just about body temperature. Any cooler you won't be able to smell much of anything from the glass; any warmer and the alcohol in Armagnac can feel very harsh. Instead of enjoying a warmth radiating downward as a sip of Armagnac makes its way down your throat to your tummy, you'll instead feel the cold alcohol burrowing a hole as it travels down your gullet. Not fun. My friend Laurent Manrique, the Gascogne chef of Aqua and the Fifth Floor in San Francisco, taught me the proper way to warm a glass of Armagnac; "*Entre les cuisses d'une femme,*" he explained, speaking like a true Frenchman.

Lychee "Bellini"

This is an Asian take on the classic Bellini, using lychees instead of the peaches. I serve this fun apéritif before an Asian-inspired dinner.

SERVES 6

14oz | 400g can Lychees in syrup
1 bottle Italian sparkling white wine, or a good Crément d'Alsace

The day before or the morning of the party, open the can of lychees and strain the syrup off the fruit, reserving both the fruit and the syrup. Set aside the lychees in a bowl, cover them well with plastic wrap, and refrigerate until ready to serve.

Pour the syrup into a container and put it in the freezer. You can use a rectangular plastic food container or even a cake pan, as long as it is deep enough to contain the syrup yet wide enough to fluff it with a fork. Once the syrup has frozen, use the tines of a fork to scrape the frozen syrup into granita-like ice flakes. Don't be too forceful, just gently scrape until the frozen syrup becomes completely flaky.

To serve, pour the wine into a flute, and top with a few lychees and a spoonful of the syrup granita.

Pruneaux à l'Armagnac: Prunes in Armagnac

In Gascony, one is not invited in for coffee but, if one is lucky, for *des pruneaux*, some prunes. Not just any regular old prune, mind you, but dried pruneaux d'Agen macerated in Armagnac. Here's a recipe so you, too, can invite your friends in for *des pruneaux*.

I serve this as a digestif. Each guest gets a tiny glass with one prune and a good pour of the Armagnac that the prunes have been soaking in. These also make a great addition to desserts. A slice of simple Madeira cake is made special with a prune and a generous douse of the Armagnac. A soft chocolate cake or, better yet, soufflé will also pair spectacularly well with prunes in Armagnac. Vanilla ice cream will do, too. I could go on, but I think I'll leave you to your imagination. Have fun.

SERVES 6

1 cup | 250ml water
scant cup | 225g sugar
1 lemon
1 vanilla pod
3 cups | 500g (unpitted) prunes, pruneaux demi-sec, *preferably from Agen*
1 bottle good Armagnac (don't use a top-shelf bottle for this, but don't go too
*   cheap either. Go for mid-range that you would definitely drink on its own.)*

Place a small saucepan over medium heat, and add water and sugar. Bring the mixture to a boil. Meanwhile, use a vegetable peeler to peel strips of rind from the lemon, and add them to the saucepan. Slice the vanilla pod in half, and drop the halves into the pan.

Bring the mixture back to a boil, and let it continue boiling for 2 minutes more. Place the prunes in a medium-sized bowl, and pour the boiling liquid over them. Cover the bowl with plastic wrap and leave the ingredients to steep for 12 hours at room temperature.

When they have finished steeping, remove the lemon peel and vanilla pod halves from the bowl. Spoon the prunes into a very large jar with a tight-fitting lid. Pour the Armagnac into the remaining liquid in the bowl, and mix well. Then pour the contents of the bowl through a sieve over the prunes in the jar. Close the jar tightly and let it stand in a cool cupboard for at least 2 weeks, or preferably 1 month, before use.

4 | How to be a fabulous foodie

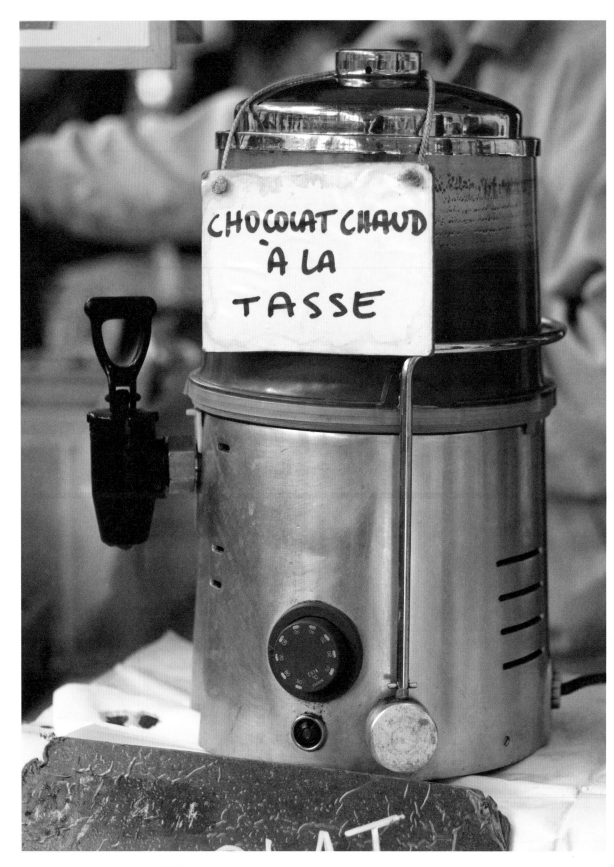

Fifty things every foodie should do, or at least try, once in her (his) life

1. Go native *(Hold the arrows! I meant go Peter Mayles's "native")*
Rent a house with a kitchen near a small market town in Italy or France for a week. Cook at least half your meals in that kitchen, using products you buy from the local markets and merchants. Dine out once a week at a bistro on the town square – the same one, and the same day of the week, every time. It doesn't matter if you don't speak a word of the local language. Take a phrase book. Better yet, take one of those with a picture you can point to next to each word so you won't even have to try pronouncing it.

2. Eat a whole roasted turbot on the Basque coast of Spain
They don't call turbot the king of fish for nothing. Throw a dart into any pile of menus from three-star Parisian restaurants and you'll hit a dish prepared with turbot. But the best way to experience the fish is to go the whole hog (well, whole fish). The fish should be so fresh it's practically still breathing, grilled over smoldering embers. An open fire, though more poetic, would just kill the delicate flavor. The only seasoning needed is salt, and perhaps a bit of olive oil. That's it really – even pepper might be overdoing it. The best way to attack a plate of roasted turbot is with your hands. Your fingers will be glued together by the gelatin in the fish flesh by the end, but you need only to lick them to release them clean again.

The best place in the world I know for this is Elkano, a fishing village about half an hour outside of San Sebastian. There, practically everything they serve comes from the sea you gaze at from your table by the window.

3. Eat a fugu

Do this preferably at a specialized restaurant that serves only fugu, most likely in Japan. The key to minimizing your risk – there is after all no known antidote to pufferfish poison – is only trust the hands of the true professionals. Look for the kind of specialist chef who serves tens of thousands of fugu a year, not a hobbyist. Or to put it bluntly, avoid the kind of hack who sees a fugu once or twice a year at best. (What, you still don't know what a fugu is? Don't even talk to me.)

4. Give up trying to like something you hate

If you truly hate the taste of something – *anything* – just don't eat it. To be a fabulous foodie is to know your own taste and to have the courage and conviction to stand by it. If you find something so repellent, why bother? If a beautiful Chioggia beetroot tastes like nothing but dirt to you, no chef in the world will be able to make it taste like something else. (Oh, no, no, no! I am not projecting or anything!) I should warn you, however, that this only works if you just have one or two (or three, to be generous) things you truly hate. If the list of stuff you hate to eat goes on for four pages, or begins with "No blue foods on Fridays,", you might want to give up being a foodie. You'll have a better shot at being a Trekkie or *Dr. Who* fan.

5. Try a durian

If not the fruit itself, at least try a dessert made from it. Millions of Southeast Asians who love the stuff can't be wrong. Or can they? Try the more refined *mon thong* or *kan yao* varieties, not the very common (and pungent) *cha nee*.

6. Dine at a Parisian three-star restaurant

Save up for it and go all out. If you have to worry about how much anything costs before ordering it, you won't have any fun. If you're in the mood to experiment, go to Pierre Gagnaire. For a meal closer to nature, where the quality of the products reigns supreme, go to

L'Arpège. The same approach with slightly more modern touches will be L'Astrance. If you want classic French food of the old school done to utter perfection, no question, L'Ambroisie. Or you can try the restaurant Le Meurice, where Yannick Alléno's cuisine is a bit more modern but still rooted in classical French cuisine.

7. Eat a perfect peach

Find a perfect, sun-drenched, tree-ripened, impossibly fragrant peach at the height of summer – so ripe it bruises just by being looked at. Bite into it; the fruit will be much juicier that way but remember to bring a spare shirt or dress. If you find yourself in Northern California during the season, go visit Andy Mariani's farm during one of his open-house days throughout summer. He has one of the largest collections of heirloom varieties of stone fruits. There, you'll definitely find a perfect peach, or two, or ten.

8. Try a stinky cheese

The stinkier the better! The current stinky cheese on the top end of my tolerance is the British farmhouse cheese called Stinking Bishop. There's truth in advertising on this one, for sure. Don't be afraid. Just try putting a piece in your mouth. You might actually like it. It's been scientifically proven that what you smell with your nose alone is different than what you smell when something is in your mouth. I guess that's why so many things that actually taste amazingly delicious smell like feet: think truffles, or, yes, stinky cheeses.

9. Find your signature dish

Find a dish you love, and then look for as many recipes for that dish as you can find. Try each of them but more than once. Craft your own version based on your experiments. Cook it over and over until you get it down pat. *Et voilà*; your signature dish. No one makes it as well as you do. Or perhaps the least you could claim is that no one does it the way you do it.

10. Try *khao chae*, in Bangkok, at the height of summer

The best time to visit Thailand and Southeast Asia is from November to February, when the climate is the most temperate. But if you go then you'll be missing *khao chae*, possibly Thai cuisine's most interesting dish.

Khao chae comprises hand-polished rice cooked al dente, floating in a pool of jasmine-scented cold water, and is served with an array of side dishes, such as stuffed sweet peppers enrobed in a delicate egg net, dried meat, stuffed shallots, fresh green mango, and many fragrant herbs. Take a spoonful of the cool rice in the fragrant water, and a bite or two of the sides. *Khao chae* is Thai cuisine at its most subtle, complex, refreshing, and intricate, hardly the usual macho make-it-hot-hot-hot Thai food you think you know. It will surprise you. You may love it. You might even hate it, but woe be the foodie who has yet to try it.

11. Sip a perfect espresso at Caffè Mulassano in Turin

Indulge in a perfectly pulled, perfectly speckled shot of espresso, with a rich, thick cream that holds a spoonful of sugar for a few seconds before letting it sink. Why the sugar? Well, everyone drinks it like that in Italy. The perfect spot is Caffè Mulassano in Turin, where the best coffee in the world is served every day. All dark wood and mirrors, with smartly dressed Italian men sipping from tiny cups while standing up at the bar, the scene is so perfect it's practically a film set labeled "Perfect Café."

12. Learn to make a perfect piecrust

Making a piecrust is not difficult. I'm not entirely sure why cook books and magazines make such a big deal of it. It's not that hard. And forget that *coagulated* vegetable shortening crap. Real foodies only ever make piecrust with butter. (See page 116 for the recipe.)

13. Take your lover on a trip to Olivier Roellinger in Cancale, Brittany

True to his Breton heritage, Olivier Roellinger is a wizard with seafood. He's also wonderful with spices, having spent his childhood playing in his grandfather's spice shop in St. Malo, the spice port of northern France. Stay in one of his properties and eat in his Michelin three-star restaurant. I promise you it will be the most romantic foodie destination of your life. My favorite is Les Rimains, which has a particular suite called Badiane occupying the lower floor of the house. Decorated in hues of blue and white, it has French doors that open out onto a green, infinite lawn that stretches out and then drops precipitously into the bay of St. Michel.

14. Go Dungeness crabbing in Washington state

Delectable Dungeness crabs are so plentiful here that, in the season, practically all you need to do is dip your shiny bucket into the water and you will pull up a few. Build a fire on the beach, steam or boil the crabs, and eat them with your fingers.

15. Pick your own berries

Pick blueberries on the coast of Maine. Pick olallieberries on the coast of Northern California. Pick wild *fraises des bois* in France. Pick English strawberries in Kent. Make sure only half of what you pick goes into the basket. The rest you should enjoy right in the moment because the best berries are at their peak right at the instant they are picked. You've got to try it to believe it.

16. Go on a quest for the best

It doesn't matter what it is. Just find something that stirs your soul, find the best place in the world for it, go there and eat it from a different restaurant or shop or vendor every day until you find the absolute best. Make a vacation of it. Search for the best *Pho* in Saigon; the best *khao soi* in Chiang Mai; the best croissant in Paris; the best pizza in Rome; the best *andouillette* in Troyes; the best *gâteau Basque* in San Sebastian. Find your own quest and, needless to say, the journey will be the destination.

17. Spend a week in New Orleans

New Orleans has the most vibrant food culture in the United States. Everyone is a foodie, and you won't find two people who can agree on the best place for gumbo or po'boy in town. Try oysters roasted over an open flame at Dragos. Try gumbo at Liuzza's by the racetracks. Try a po'boy just about everywhere and then make up your own mind. New Orleans is a proud city still struggling to get back to her feet after having been devastated by Hurricane Katrina. Go there, eat the food, spend the money, and revel in the *Laissez les bons temps rouler!* attitude of that town. That's how you can do your part to help, and you'll have a lot of fun doing it, too.

18. Score a table at elBulli

Yes, I meant to say score a table at elBulli rather than have a meal at elBulli. The restaurant is only open from April to September. The rest of the time the chef and his crew spend in a laboratory, working out recipes for the next season. For the 8,000 or so available dinner seats each season, elBulli receives close to half a million reservation requests. The odds are stacked against you but that's why it's such a thrill. However, I'll pass on a little trick I learned from my friend Louisa Chu. The reservation book opens each year on October 15. It's important to fax or e-mail your request. Don't leave a message on their answering machine. (In fact, I don't think they have an answering machine.) Just don't call, period. Oh, and hey, I'll let you in on another little secret. I've eaten at elBulli but I have never managed to score a table there on my own yet. I should take my own advice and try for next year.

19. Cook without recipes

The late Alain Chapel, a chef's chef if there ever was one, likened recipes to prison for the cooking mind. My friend Daniel Patterson, the chef and owner of Coi in San Francisco, says it's like driving your car with a GPS on. You may get where you need to go, but you won't be able to return on your own. Blindly following recipes prevents you from getting the feel of the food and the cooking, stops you from honing your cooking instincts and from understanding what works and why.

Now, I'm not telling you never to look at another recipe, or buy another cook book, but just let loose once in a while and cook following your instincts. Let go. You might burn a chicken or two, but you might also end up with the best chicken you've ever had in your entire life. You never know until you've tried it.

20. Learn to make an easy but decadent chocolate cake

Here's how. You will need 7oz/200g good plain chocolate, chopped or broken into small pieces; 1 cup/225g butter; 1/4 cup/25g cocoa powder; 5 large eggs, separated; 1 cup/225g sugar; 1/2 cup/60g flour; 1/4 cup/85g soured cream (or crème fraîche); and a pinch of salt.

Put the chocolate, butter, and cocoa powder in a medium-sized glass bowl. Microwave for one or two minutes, depending on the power of your machine, just until the butter and about half of the chocolate have melted. Remove the bowl from the microwave and stir until everything is mixed together. Set aside. Put the yolks, sugar, and flour in another medium-sized glass bowl and stir with a spatula or a wooden spoon until well mixed. Add the crème fraîche and salt and stir until blended. Pour this mixture into the bowl with the melted chocolate and butter mixture, and stir to blend well. Set aside. Whisk the egg whites using your own amazing elbow grease, or a stand or handheld mixer. Beat until the egg whites form a soft peak, that is to say, it forms a peak that quickly leans over to one side as you pull the whisk up from the whipped cloud. Take about one-third of the whipped whites and whisk it into the batter until well mixed. Fold the rest gently into the batter until the white streaks entirely disappear into the chocolate batter.

Preheat the oven to 400°F/200°C/Gas Mark 6. Butter and flour a 9-by-15-inch/22-by-12-cm loaf pan, and line it with parchment paper. Pour in the chocolate batter and use the back of a knife to level the surface a bit. Bake in the oven for 25 to 30 minutes until the surface has a little bounce. Remove the cake from the oven, but leave it in the pan, and let cool in the pan on the countertop for about an hour. Wrap the whole thing in aluminum foil and refrigerate. Remove it from the fridge at least an hour before serving, and run a knife between the cake and the sides of the pan. Remove the cake from the pan onto a plate and slice. You can serve this with fresh berries, preserves, or a dollop of whipped cream. This will be your default chocolate cake from now on. If you want a bit of variety, you can bake this batter in muffin tins – or other fancy single-serving shapes – for 12 to 15 minutes.

21. Buy some kitchen scales

The way to properly measure something and make it the same every time is by weight. Professional cooks and bakers already know this. It's going to eventually trickle down to home cooks and consumer cook books. You might as well get in ahead of the pack. Plus, you will never need to wash another measuring cup again.

22. Learn how to cook your mom's (or dad's) best dish

Even the least foodie-like mom has a dish she does superbly. Learn how to make it just the way she did. One day you'll be thankful you did, and so will the generation after you.

23. Eat a Yangcheng hairy crab, preferably in or near Yangcheng Lake in China

Hairy crabs are one of the great Chinese delicacies. They are not totally hairy, just hairy around the legs. They have an extraordinary flavor that's difficult to describe. I would just say that its reputation as a great delicacy is absolutely deserved. However, after the meal, don't forget to drink ginger tea, or have a dessert featuring ginger. Hairy Crabs are very high in Yang energy, and ginger, a Yin food, will help balance it. You'll catch a cold otherwise. Trust me on this.

24. Throw a Locavore party

The Locavores (www.locavores.com) are a group of concerned culinary adventurers who make the effort to eat only foods grown or harvested within a 100-mile/160-kilometer radius of their home in San Francisco. You can do the same by drawing up a list of what's available and in season in your area. You may not think that there are very many things to offer, but I am sure you'll be surprised once you start looking into farms and food producers in the prescribed radius. Plan a dinner party for your friends, and make sure more than 80 percent of the products you buy for the party are local. Print out a list of the products, and producers you bought them from, and send it home with your guests.

25. Throw a Pad Thai party with your friends

Invite a group of friends round and follow my Pad Thai "recipe" on page 67. Make a special trip to your local Asian market to procure all the ingredients. Prepare the sauce a day ahead and organize the rest of the ingredients on the day of the party. (Better yet, assign each ingredient to a friend so that the rather heavy prep work is not all done by you and you alone. Line up all your ingredients in a close reach of the wok. (You do have a wok, yes?) Make sure you have a continuous flow of Champagne or good Riesling to keep your friends occupied while waiting their turn at the noodles. Start cooking your Pad Thai one or two portions at a time. Friends who are brave enough could even do it themselves.

26. Try a can of aged sardines

Harold McGee, a preeminent food scientist, told me he had quite a few cans stashed away. Apparently, something amazing takes place in that vacuum environment of the can, where the fat, acid, and protein inside interact to develop an amazing flavor.

27. Feast on oysters

There are many famous varieties of oysters, such as the Belon oysters of Brittany. You may also have heard of the *fine de claire* oysters from Marennes (frankly, those are too thick and meaty for me. I prefer the more delicate *la pousse en claire*, even more so than I do the Belon.) On the U.S. East Coast, nothing can beat the small Pemaquid oysters from Maine, while on the West Coast, my favorites are the tiny *kumamotos*.

Superb, supremely fresh oysters need no embellishment at all. Even a squeeze of fresh lime is perhaps overdoing it. If you really want to, you can make a mignonette sauce to accompany your oysters, using a few chopped shallots, some sherry vinegar, and a little salt and pepper. To me it's a distraction, but a delicious one nevertheless. While you are at it, read *The Big Oyster* by Mark Kurlansky for practically everything you need to know about oysters.

In London, the Wright Brothers at Borough Market introduced me to the fabulous West Mersea native oysters from Clochester, where oysters have been harvested since the times of the Romans. They are ever so delicate, with their amazing mineral quality making them an even more perfect match with a superb Chablis than most French oysters.

28. Try a famous Japanese kobe beef steak

You want the real Japanese stuff: "American" kobe doesn't count. Australian Kobe is a bit better, but frankly it doesn't count either. The magnificence of Japanese Kobe beef is not only its flavor but also the

melting, buttery texture produced by the muscles, which are well marbled with fat. A kobe steak should be cooked to about medium to make sure that the temperature of the meat is high enough to begin to melt the fat, which gives the juiciest, tastiest meat flavor.

In many restaurants in the United States, Kobe has become a code word for really great and – perhaps more important – expensive meat that is sold to unwitting customers with deep pockets. From there sprang such hideous culinary creations as the kobe burger or kobe meatloaf. This is like searching out the best gelato in Rome, putting it in a glass, and leaving it in the sun until it has melted, and then drinking it, fully expecting it to have just as much flavor and texture as when it was first scooped out for you at the gelatería.

29. Eat a wild bird during game season in Europe

It doesn't really matter what kind of game you try: pheasant, partridge, grouse or palombe, just find one with a bit of lead shot still in it. You should like really, really gamey flavors, though. It's not going to taste like chicken, that's what I should say. I once had a grouse at St. John in London that had been hung to just this side of putrid, roasted ever so gently so the skin was crisp but the inside was still practically blue. The flavor was amazing, but frankly I wasn't so sure I would live after finishing it.

30. Find your favorite prawn in the world

Try all the best varieties of prawn in the world, such as *gambas rojas* from the Alicante coast of Spain, *gambero rosso* from northern Italy, or pink Greenland shrimp from (you guessed it) Greenland, or gorgeously speckled spot prawns from Santa Barbara, California. Learn the story of each variety, how they are harvested, and how they are best cooked and enjoyed. Keep a set of tasting notes, compare them and then choose a favorite. Compose a paragraph singing its praises, especially emphasizing how all the others pale in comparison. Memorize it. Then, use it to dominate the conversation at a party, especially when someone tries to out-foodie you. Just counter them with "So, what's your favorite kind of prawn?" You will win every time.

31. Taste Osetra caviar, the real stuff, from Iran

Do it soon because it won't last much longer. You will be telling your grandchildren about it one day.

32. Make a *torchon de foie gras* and serve it as a canapé

Preferably with a great wine to accompany it. One of the best and most thorough recipes can be found in the *French Laundry Cook Book*. Yes, yes, I know nobody cooks from that book, but if there's one recipe you should try, it has to be this one.

33. Make your lover an omelette buried under thin shavings of black truffles

Take one perfect black truffle from France, brush the dirt from the skin, and leave it in a closed container with 4 eggs. Of course, your truffles will still have dirt on the skin. Truffles begin to deteriorate as soon as they are parted from the dirt covering, so great truffles are always shipped covered in the dirt they have been dug up in. Mediocre truffles, like mediocre caviar and cut-price Champagne, are just not worth bothering with. So, you do this with the best truffles, or you don't do it at all. A perfectly made omelette with perfectly fresh-farmed eggs is a beauty in itself, don't defile it with ordinary truffles.

The next morning, brush any remaining dirt from the truffle. Get your truffle shaver out onto the worktop at the ready. Crack the eggs into a bowl and lightly whip with a fork. Beat the eggs just to combine the whites and yolks and to whip a little air into the mixture. You don't need to work very hard on this. Notice I haven't said salt, not yet.

Heat a perfectly seasoned 8-inch/20-cm cast-iron pan over medium-high heat. You can use a nonstick pan if that makes you feel a bit more confident. Heat the pan until hot but not smoking. Melt a tablespoon of butter into the pan and quickly add the beaten eggs. Let the eggs sit in the pan for 10 to 20 seconds, until they are beginning to cook, hardening at the bottom and around the side of the pan. Using the side of a fork, starting from one edge of the pan, pull the egg about one-third of the way in toward the middle. You should see a layer of cooked egg wrinkles and folds, like a hastily pulled curtain. Tilt the pan toward the side you've just pulled the egg from to let liquid, uncooked egg flow in to replace the part you've just pulled up. Do this again, going around the circle of the pan, until you only have a thin layer of uncooked, liquid egg on top, and you have the folds and wrinkles from the egg being pulled around the pan.

Grab the truffle and the shaver and quickly shave a good dose of truffle on top of the omelette. Fold the omelette twice from opposite sides, each toward the middle. Grab a good chunk of butter, salted butter this time, and rub that baby all over the top of the cooked, folded omelette. Don't be shy – indulgence and diet don't go together. Sprinkle a bit of fleur de sel on top of everything if you want it salty. Shave more truffle on top of the still-warm omelette. Black truffles need a bit of heat to accentuate their aroma, so it's important that you work quickly so the omelette doesn't get cold before getting kissed by the truffles. Serve immediately, preferably in bed. A little Champagne wouldn't hurt either.

By the way, I suggest neither of you plan to be productive that morning. The Greeks and Romans believed truffles are a major aphrodisiac, and so do I.

34. Eat a plate of *truffe bel humeur* at the restaurant L'Ambroisie in Paris

The finest black truffles come from Périgord and are best when gently, indirectly heated, which lifts the already strong aroma into the territory of intoxication. The best example of truffles I have ever eaten is perhaps *truffe bel humeur*, at L'Ambroisie. My friend Julien Port said it best, "A whole truffle cut in two like a burger bun, a thick slice of foie gras inside, puff pastry around the whole thing, truffle sauce underneath. Amen."

35. Eat a perfectly made risotto covered with white truffles from Alba

There's nothing else to say about this: just perfectly made rice with fresh white truffles. If you're on the Côte d'Azur, be sure to buy the truffles from the Truffle Don. Look him up; tell him I sent you. Otherwise, find the best white truffles you could afford. Then make a perfect risotto, and cover it with even more perfect shavings of white truffles. (Check out the risotto recipe on page 106. Just forget the part about the licorice and other flavorings and make a plain risotto with rice, broth, and cheese.)

36. Have an *omakase* meal at one of the best sushi-ya in the world

The concept of *omakase* is based on trust, as you trust the chef to give you the very best. Go to one of the best sushi bars in the world and trust the chef. Try Masa in New York, Urasawa in Beverly Hills, or Mizutani in Tokyo.

37. Throw out your entire spice rack and start all over again

Spices only have shelf life of about six months. How long have your spices been there? If you're anything like my foodie friends, they've probably been there quite a lot longer. Chances are you never used more than five or six spices in the set of thirty you bought anyway. Throw them all out and start anew. Only purchase the types of spices you actually use so that you can afford to buy better quality.

38. Have all your knives professionally sharpened or buy a good knife

Every American cook worth their fleur de sel seems to have a collection of knives, starting from a blade of 6-inch (15-cm) or 8-inch (21-cm) or even 10-inch (25-cm) chef's knife. You know, to some people, size matters. To be honest, I'm not one of them. The knife I use most often is not a regular chef's knife, but a smaller, all-purpose Japanese knife. Just find one or two knives that feel the most comfortable in your hand. If you select a chef's knife, that's great. If not, that's fine, too. However, whatever you end up using, make sure your knives are always sharp. Have them professionally sharpened occasionally, and you'll be pleasantly pleased at the results.

39. Buy a cast-iron frying pan

The only way to cook a piece of steak in your kitchen and make it worth eating is on a cast-iron frying pan. Buy one and once you're accustomed to it, you'll be using it for all kinds of things.

40. Cook a dish based on a spice (or spice blend) you don't know

Try something new to you, such as *raz al hanout* or *vadouvan* curry. Just try. David said to try *vadouvan*, a fermented curry paste, with roasted lamb chops. It's not the most obvious pairing in the world, but you'll be surprised.

41. Hold an olive oil tasting

Don't just buy random bottles from the shop and taste them. Do some research about olive varieties, regional styles, and great producers from around the world. Get a few select bottles that are representative of distinct styles and varieties. For example, buy a bottle of *arbequina* olive oil from Catalonia, a bottle of *taggiasca* from Liguria, *picual* from Spain, and mission from California. Do a comparison tasting of them and find out which one you favor and why. Once you find a particular variety or region you like, then you can do another tasting with different producers from that region to find one you like best.

42. Bake a loaf of crusty bread
See "How to bake bread" (page 207).

43. Volunteer at a soup kitchen or donate to the U.N. World Food Programme
There are hungry people in this world. We are lucky not to be one of them. Just remember that, and help them. Oh, yes, and next time, finish the leftovers in your fridge, too.

44. Eat in the street in Asia
For beginners, go to one of the hawker markets in Singapore where you will find sanitized street food. Okay, you'll be missing some of the fun (and the bacteria), but if you're just starting out it will be perfect. Plus, it's hard to argue with a delicious plate or two of *char kua tiew*. Once you muster up enough courage to move beyond the sparkling-clean hawker stalls, fly an hour north to Bangkok and go to one of the bigger, more touristy markets like Or Tor Kor. Don't eat the bugs, though. They're mostly there as a dare for tourists to eat them, but make a beeline to one of the pig stalls selling every part of every size of pig. Try the skin-on belly, which is steamed and then flash-fried to crisp up the skin. When you get braver still, visit markets in the countryside of Thailand or, better yet, try Laos, Vietnam or Cambodia. Though I'd still stay away from the bugs.

45. Have tea at Mariage Frères in Paris
Observe the white-uniformed, white-gloved tea brewers behind the bar at this wonderful place. These guys take tea more seriously than anyone we know. Each tea is brewed at a certain temperature and for a precise length of time, and then decanted immediately into another pot to stop the tea from steeping.

46. Eat a taco while standing up at a taco truck

If you're a truly Absolutely Fabulous foodie, when in California have a ceviche, standing up, at a taco truck, preferably one with no running water.

47. Order the Menu du Jardin at L'Arpège

No one quite has a way with vegetables the way Alain Passard does. That's hardly surprising, considering that the "cooking" doesn't begin in the kitchen, but traces its roots far beyond Paris to his own farms in Brittany and Normandy, where the suprelative produces were grown the old-fashioned way. On the plates at the Michelin three-star restaurant, freshly pulled carrots are paired with an intriquing chocolate sauce made savory with an infusion of lobster jus. Sweetest green peas float in a bowl of delicate onion broth and tart grapefruit. It's expensive, yes, but you're not just paying for the peas, you are paying for the whole philosophy and intricacy behind it. If that's worth something to you, you might have the best meal of your life. If not, take a pass on this one.

48. Send back dishes made with truffles in the summer

Flavorless, flimsy summer truffles don't do very much for any dish, though they could do quite a lot to your bill. I'm almost convinced chefs only use them to add the perception of luxury to their fancy restaurants. Say no to mediocrity and send it back.

49. Try something "molecular" in your cooking

Molecular gastronomy is creeping out of fancy Michelin-star kitchens and heading closer and closer to our home kitchen. Put yourself back in science class again. Have a go at playing with agar agar powder or some dry ice or liquid nitrogen and see if you can change the texture or flavor of the food you are cooking in novel, even bizarre, ways. It's going to be fun. A great place to start is Heston Blumenthal's *In Search of Perfection* book. Try his pizza recipe – it's fantastic.

50. Have a pig roast party

Picture this: a grassy hilltop under the shade of ancient oak trees surrounded by lush vineyards; a big, delicious, rare-breed, once-happily-roaming-outside pig slowly roasting on an open fire until the meat is meltingly soft and the skin crisp; good wines; you and your friends lounging on the green grass in the cool autumn breeze; the ocean shimmering right over that far ridge over there.

Tell your friends to arrive hungry and to bring a side dish to share, as well as something else to throw on the grill should they not want to partake in the *fête de cochon*. They can always bring wine or beer if their cooking is not for public consumption (there can never be enough wine).

Just so there's no need to resort to disposable things, advise your friends to bring their own plates, wine/water glasses, and utensils (but don't be offended if they decide to use their hands).

How to be an ethical foodie

You let out a sigh just reading the title, didn't you? How positively boring, and how daunting, too! Most people throw their hands up in the air and just give up. It's not even that being an ethical foodie is hard, but most of us can't even figure out what exactly being an ethical foodie is to begin with.

We all pretty much agree on the simple principle that living a greener life is better for us and for our environment. (I mean, yes, you agree with that, right? Because otherwise we've got to start from an entirely different place, and I'm not sure I have enough room in these pages for that. Go watch *An Inconvenient Truth* or read *The Omnivore's Dilemma* and then get back to me.) Moreover, for us foodies, the proof is on the proverbial plate. Industrially, conventionally grown strawberries in January, shipped over to us from goodness-knows-where, cannot possibly compete with the delights of those sun-kissed, locally grown, freshly picked berries we buy from farmers' markets at the height of summer. Free-range farm chickens pack the flavor and pleasing texture entirely missing from the flabby, waterlogged, intensively farmed chickens that probably never spent a day of their short lives under the open sky.

The problem is not that we don't believe green is good, but the messages in the media about what exactly qualifies as "green" and "ethical" can confuse even those of us with the best intentions. We are told organic is good (we ingest fewer pesticides), and that eating organically grown food is better for our environment (less chemical residue left in the land). We learn that eating locally grown food might even be better. All those food miles spent hauling fresh raspberries, organic or otherwise, from Chile or Peru to our supermarkets in January leave an enormous carbon footprint.

So, we aim to buy locally grown food first, organic second. Well, to be honest, that's where things get complicated. The organic-over-local proponents argue that growing produce in a less hospitable environment (for example, the United Kingdom in February) consumes even more energy and leaves a bigger carbon footprint than bringing in organic rice from Vietnam. They also argue that the buy-local movement harms poor farmers and food producers in developing countries: what would impoverished rice farmers in Vietnam do without the rice export market?

Some retailers have even tried to "help" by either listing their carbon footprint on the package, or specifying that they are planting trees to compensate for their carbon emission. Alas, these are still far from useful, at least in the current state. There's still no agreed standard on where to draw the line when calculating the numbers. What's the carbon emission of an ear of corn? Do you count all the carbon-emitting practices at the farm on which it was grown? Or do you go even further back to count the emission of the share of fertilizer used in the production of that ear as well? Things get even more complicated when companies try to offset their carbon emission by paying to have a tree planted, for example. These offsets create absurd scenarios where a brand of bottled water that's shipped all the way from a South Pacific island to destinations in Europe and North America can somehow claim negative carbon emission. Without a standard for calculating carbon emissions in food produce it is very confusing for consumers. However, these efforts to do something are better than doing nothing at all.

On top of all this confusion are those skeptics who call us all elitist do-gooders who are merely green-washing our lifestyle in order to appease our yuppie, consumerist guilt. They accuse us of looking down our noses at the great unwashed, such as those who carry plastic bags and consume non-free-range eggs. Give each side a soapbox and send each one to their own corner in Hyde Park. They'll still be arguing their case by the time the polar ice caps melt down completely. And then instead of standing on their boxes, they'll be using them as a floatation device to keep from drowning, just so they can go on arguing.

So, yes, you could just hold out and wait for the definitive verdict on what's best to do before you actually do anything, but I wouldn't hold my breath. That ultimate verdict may never arrive at all. Or we could start today and do what we can now.

Ten easy ways to become a (more) ethical foodie

1. Buy in bulk A big part of energy used during transport is wasted on excess packaging for products rather than the products themselves. Even if you only buy products packaged in recyclable containers, it still uses up energy to transport the containers and more energy in the recycling. If you have enough storage room at home, buy the biggest

packets of anything you need, then use small reusable containers to portion them out for use. If you don't have room, you might share and split the cost of those items with a few friends. Food items that could go stale might not be ideal if you live alone, but household items like soap, shampoo, or dishwashing detergent will easily keep for a long time.

2. Shop locally, seasonally, and organically where you can Support your local agriculture and artisan producers by buying more seasonal and locally produced food. Take an inventory of your cupboard and find out how far all those ingredients must have traversed to get there. If you can find local producers that make those products just as – or even more – deliciously, switch to using them instead. No one is telling you to give up drinking coffee or eating rice unless they are grown within a hundred miles of where you live, just do what you can. Also, look for sustainable or organically produced products to replace conventional products you normally buy. Even if you only make one or two changes, every little bit counts.

3. Say no to the question "paper or plastic?" Take your own shopping bag, basket, or those handy wheelies you see everyone using at Parisian street markets. Why use those awful-looking paper bags or those noisy, ugly, droopy plastic bags when you can accessorize with a gorgeous bag or a cool basket? Mother Earth will thank you.

4. Drink tap water   Plastic water bottles take up a huge amount of room in landfill – and probably last just about forever there, too. Why add to that waste when you can drink perfectly safe water right there from the tap in your home? And the best bit – it's even free. If you have a strong aversion to the – at times – funky aroma of chlorine in tap water, look into getting a water filter that you can fit onto your tap. I bought one last year and have been using it ever since. I'm not sure if I could tell the difference in flavor now between the water from my filtered tap and that from a plastic bottle. And I'm pretty sure neither would you.

5. Volunteer for a day at an organic farm   Working with your hands in the dirt, getting up close and personal with where your food comes from, will give you an insight into the growing processes and a brand-new respect for the food you eat. You could even make a visit to one of those "pick your own" farms and try your hands at harvesting a few pounds of berries. You might gain a whole new appreciation for food from the experience: love it more, waste less of it. You might even become a better cook in the process.

6. Make a fridge soup once a week   Try cooking a meal using only what you have in your fridge. It doesn't have to be soup precisely, just anything that will use up the food that has been lingering almost too long in your fridge. You know, that bunch of basil you bought specifically for a pasta you did last week? Or that sad-looking, slightly wilted head of lettuce that you had in a salad a few days ago? Use only what you have – no running to the corner shop to buy a bunch of parsley or a pint of milk. Just improvise with what you've got, don't follow a recipe. You will improve your cooking instincts to no end and you will be doing your part to stem the enormous amount of global kitchen waste, all at once.

7. Use greener cleaners in your kitchen   Who wants all those scary chemicals so near the source of food you will be ingesting anyway? You can go green by buying biodegradable cleaners. You can even mix your own if you have the time and the inclination: ordinary vinegar and baking soda will clean just about everything that needs cleaning in your kitchen.

8. Go for cloth, not paper   I stopped buying paper towels cold turkey, and I've been on the no-paper-towel wagon for nearly six months as I'm writing this. It's not that difficult, really, just try. Use cloth napkins at mealtimes, you'll not only be stepping lightly on the earth but a little more elegantly as well.

9. Unplug the appliances on your counter   A toaster, a coffeemaker, a kettle, a blender, perhaps a food processor, what else do you have plugged in permanently on your countertop? While plugged in, appliances continue to draw power even when they are not on. Unplug them.

10. Help others who are still hungry   If you're holding this book, you're one of those lucky people for whom food is not simple sustenance but also an indulgence. So, it would be nice, at least once in a while, to think about those who don't share our luxury. Hunger is still a very real and present problem in the world. If you have a chance, do your part to help. There are many organizations working to help solve world hunger: the U.N. World Food Programme is one. I run a fundraiser called Menu for Hope each December on my blog, Chez Pim, to help support their laudable efforts. You can donate directly to them at http://wfp.org. If you don't feel like giving "hand-outs," you can support food-based businesses by becoming a micro-lender with Kiva. Go to http://kiva.org and run a search for food-based business Kiva will help link you directly to an entrepreneur in the developing world in need of funding.

Go ahead, change one thing you can. Right now. Make a promise to yourself or your personal god and just commit to changing one thing. It can be anything. Go out and buy a cool bag for your next shopping trip. Or pick something else from this list, perhaps. Find something you can change straightaway and do it. It doesn't matter how big or small it is. Just do it. Yes, now would be the time.

Cook your story

"I remember the perfume that filled the house when my grandmère made her white peach jam every summer," said Alain Passard as he chewed on a piece of fragrant dried white peach from a farm we visited earlier that day. "How extraordinary," he murmured – whether he was savoring the delicious mouthful in the present or it was the phantom of his grandmother's jam in his mind I did not know for certain. He was so blissfully lost in his thoughts that I did not want to intrude with a question. It was a glorious afternoon. We sat basking in the California sun in the garden after a light lunch with a few friends. On the menu was a taste from my own lost childhood, *kanom jeen nam-prik*, an old Thai dish with fermented rice noodle and a mild "curry" sauce made with prawns and coconut milk.

Cooking, as Alain said that afternoon while we lounged in the gentle breeze, is meant to be evocative. For some, like us, the story is a perpetual journey to rediscover the tastes from our past. Alain often talks of his grandmother Louise, who had an immense influence on his life and work, and to whom he credited many recipes in use today at his Parisian three-star L'Arpège. "*Recette de ma grandmère*," he would say with palpable pride. As for me, my influence was my grandfather, Khunta as I called him in Thai, whose taste and passion for food I take after.

Re-creating an old Thai dish from my past is the shortest path back to those languid summer days on my grandfather's patio. The best cooks tell stories with food, whether it is a retelling of one's past or an adventurous quest to conquer something new. Learning to cook your story is a sure path to become a fabulous foodie. Find your story, let it drive you to explore deeper into the world of food. That's how you get better and keep from being bored.

My foodie story is about bringing the present into focus. When I cook Thai food in California, I think of ways to use and adapt local produce to achieve the flavors I remember from the past. I dislike using preserved or canned ingredients to stay true to a recipe. Often, the real flavors of those ingredients – the heart of the matter for me – have long disappeared somewhere in the process of preservation or transport. No, I'm not against using canned or frozen coconut milk, since the flavors I am looking for are still largely there. But for more delicate ingredients, I prefer to stick to the spirit of the recipe rather than the letter.

That is how I've come to create this recipe for one of my favorite dishes called *kanom jeen nam-prik*. The ingredient list for this "curry" is long and full of hard-to-find ingredients. It calls for *ra-gum*, an odd fruit whose English name I don't even know, for the sour, fruity flavor; *Bai Thong Laang*, a bitter leaf that is battered, deep-fried, and served as a condiment for the noodles and curry; and shredded green mango, among others. Here in California, during the summer I use sour plums as a substitute for the *ra-gum* fruit, and in the winter a Granny Smith apple. The "curry" sauce relies on freshwater prawns, that make for a delicious sauce. I often use flavorful spot prawns, which are sustainably fished just off the Monterey coast. In place of the bitter *bai thong laang*, I use spinach or any other bitter leaves, often picked right from the garden. Battered and deep-fried, they provide the crunch and slight bite that complement the creamy sauce very well. I even add my own twist, using pungent *shiso* leaves to add yet another interesting dimension to the dish.

With these adjustments, I've transformed an old Thai dish into a quintessentially Californian adaptation while keeping the spirit of the recipe. I also made a dessert that afternoon with Alain, a simple *Loy Gaew* (page 140), with local citrus (from Gene Lester's farm) floating in a refreshing iced ginger syrup. Even the French chef was impressed. I caught him drinking the last bit of sauce directly from the bowl. "You could open a restaurant, Pim," Alain said, looking up from his food just long enough to wink at me. I smiled back at him. My Khunta would be proud.

Kanom jeen nam-prik

Rice noodles with prawn nam-prik sauce

The classic accompaniments to this Thai dish, *kanom jeen nam-prik*, are batter-fried vegetables, blanched wing beans cut into thin slices, green mango or papaya cut into matchsticks, deep-fried sliced shallots and garlic, and deep-fried dried chiles. These may look daunting, but they are practically all optional. The *nam-prik* is good even eaten just with some noodles or over rice, but adding the accompaniments, with the layer of textures and flavors will add a lot to the dish. Serve these accompaniments on a separate plate. Your guests can take a little of this and that to their own taste at the table.

In Thailand we use *kanom jeen*, which are long, thin noodles made from fermented rice dough, but you can easily use dried Japanese tomoshiraga noodles instead. Tomoshiraga noodles are white and the thickness of angel hair pasta. They are widely available in Asian shops and can even be ordered online. If your local Chinese market carries Vietnamese *bun xio* noodles, you can use them as an alternative.

SERVES 4 (OR MORE IF PART OF A MULTICOURSE MEAL)

SAUCE
19oz | 540ml can coconut milk
1/2 cup | 120ml water
3/4 cup | 150g (dried) mung beans
1/2 cup | 25g shredded coconut, tightly packed
1/2 cup | 75g unsalted roasted peanuts
4 tablespoons vegetable oil,
1 1/2 tablespoons chili powder
1 1/2 lb | 700g prawns
4 tablespoons palm sugar
about 6 tablespoons fish sauce (nam pla)
juice of 1 lime

PASTE
2 medium-sized shallots
2 large garlic cloves
1/2-inch | 1cm small round piece of galangal root
1 teaspoon kosher salt

FOR THE BATTER

1 cup | *150g rice flour*
$^1/4$ cup | *25g plain flour*
1 teaspoon baking powder
$1^1/2$ teaspoons salt
1 teaspoon sugar
1 cup | *225ml soda water*

oil for frying battered greens (I use canola, but any mild-flavored, high-heat
    oil will do)
2 loose leaves of leafy greens, such as spinach or rocket
4 to 5 garlic cloves
4 to 5 small shallots
small handful of dried chiles
1 small Granny Smith apple, peeled and cut into matchsticks
1 handful of green beans, cooked and cut into thin rounds
Thai kanom jeen *noodles, Japanese* tomoshiraga *noodles, or Vietnamese*
    bun xio *noodles*

Start off the *nam-prik* sauce by skimming off $^1/2$ cup/120ml of the creamy part from the can of coconut milk and setting it aside. Pour the rest into a medium-sized pot. Add the water to the pot. Heat up the mixture until it is bubbly. Then lower the heat, add the mung beans, and let it simmer gently.

Meanwhile, heat up a wok over medium-low heat until it is hot, add the shredded coconut and stir it vigorously for about 3 to 5 minutes, until the white coconut flesh turns brown. (You must keep stirring or the coconut will burn.) Transfer the roasted coconut to a plate, and set it aside.

Now work on the paste by roasting the shallots, garlic, and galangal. If you are cooking with gas you can thread them onto long skewers and hold them over an open flame on the stove until they are completely blackened on the outside. Or you can place them in an oven at 450°F/230°C/Gas Mark 8 for 10 minutes. Once they have cooled, peel and discard the darkened skin. Chop them finely and place them in a mortar with the kosher salt. Pound everything to a fine paste. Transfer the paste to a small bowl and set it aside.

In the same mortar, pound the peanuts for the *nam-prik* into bits a little larger than the size of the mung beans. They don't have to be uniform in size, so some larger bits will be just fine. Just don't pound them into peanut butter. Then set them aside.

Wipe the coconut bits out of the wok and put it back on the stove. Pour in the vegetable oil and when it is hot, add the shallot/garlic/galangal paste and stir it vigorously for 1 to 2 minutes until it is very fragrant. Add the 1/2 cup/120ml of coconut cream you reserved earlier. Cook the cream and the paste together, stirring frequently, until you can see a layer of oil breaking out from the mixture. Continue cooking until more oil breaks out. This should take about 3 to 5 minutes. Then add the chili powder, beginning with 2 teaspoons (you can add more later if you want to). Stir well for 30 seconds and then turn the heat off.

Reserve one-third of the prawns and set them aside. Put the rest of the prawns into the pot in which the mung beans are cooking. Add the cooked chili paste and stir it in well. Add the ground peanuts, and the roasted coconut. Bring the pot back to simmering. Then turn the heat off and use a hand blender to blend the content of the pot. You don't need a fine purée. Just keep blending until you have a rough sauce. (If you don't have a hand blender, you can use a stand blender but do the blending in small batches so you do not burn yourself.)

Add the reserved whole prawns and season with palm sugar and fish sauce. Taste the mixture carefully because various brands of palm sugar and fish sauce will have a different intensity. You want the *nam-prik* mixture in the pot to taste slightly sweet and then salty. Make sure that the seasoning balance is intense enough because you won't be eating this sauce by the spoonful by itself, but tossed with bland noodles. Add more fish sauce or palm sugar if needed.

Turn the heat off and add the lime juice. Taste it to see if there is enough acidity. If not, add a little more. If it is too acidic, add a bit more fish sauce and sugar (granulated sugar is fine at this point). The mixture should taste sweet, sour, salty, and with a little kick of the chili at the end. (The *nam-prik* can be prepared ahead until this point and kept overnight. It will lose some of the brightness of the lime, so you should add a little bit more after you reheat the sauce just before serving it. Then sprinkle the rest of the coconut over the *nam-prik* just before serving, and give it a quick stir.)

Now you can make the accompaniments, if you are serving them. To make the batter for the fried accompaniments, mix all the dry ingredients in a medium bowl. Add about two-thirds of the soda water, and whisk until incorporated. What you're looking for here is for the batter to have the consistency of thick cream, but not quite thick enough to be yogurt. Add the rest of the water if needed. You may need a bit more or a tad less than the amount specified in the recipe.

For the frying oil, fill a saucepan or wok until the oil comes up to at least 2 inches/5cm from the bottom. The more oil you use, the higher temperature in the cooking. Place the pan over high heat until hot. Flick a few drops of batter into the pan to test the readiness. If the batter bits float to the surface and sizzle right away, your oil is ready. If not, let the oil heat up a bit more. It's important to make sure the oil is hot enough, otherwise everything will come out limp and sodden.

HOW TO BE A FABULOUS FOODIE

Dip the leaves into the batter and then drop them, gently, into the hot oil. It's important to do only a few pieces at a time so as not to lower the temperature in the pan too much. Fry until each piece is golden brown on all sides. Drain on a plate lined with a clean tea towel (not terrycloth) or paper towels for a couple of minutes before serving.

The slight bitterness from the greens and the crunch from the fried batter will add another layer of complexity to the dish. I also like to slice a couple of shallots (thinly and lengthwise, and a few cloves of garlic, then fry them until brown and crispy. Don't fry the garlic and shallots together because they take different lengths of time to cook. If you don't like the taste of fried garlic and shallots, just skip them.

Before you throw out the oil you used for the batter, fry up a handful of small dried chiles as well. Just fry them very briefly until the chile pods puff up and change color slightly. They will add a nice kick when crumpled up into the dish. Allowing each of your guests to add their own chile enables them to control the level of spiciness on their plate.

Use a Granny Smith apple, cut into matchsticks, instead of green mango or papaya, which could be hard to find. The matchsticks add freshness and acidity to the dish. You can also cook a handful of green beans and serve them in little thinly sliced rounds.

Now, cook your noodles. Place a medium-sized pot full of water over high heat on the stove and bring it to a boil. Put the noodles into the water. Cook *tomoshiraga* noodles for 2 minutes (or if using *bun xio* noodles, cook for 1 minute), then drain, and serve immediately.

At the table, your guests should each place a serving of noodles in their bowl, pour on a ladle of the *nam-prik* sauce, then add the accompaniments to taste. This dish should be eaten the traditional Thai way, by pushing the food into your spoon with your fork and then eating from the spoon.

How to bake bread

Or how to find your culinary obsession

Jim Lahey and Mark Bittman's co-accomplishment in the culinary world is such that it now can be divided into the Pre No-knead (PrN) period and the Post No-knead (PoN) period. When Mark Bittman published the recipe in the *New York Times*, it caused a sensation. Home cooks who'd dared not touch yeast bread were found stirring up sticky dough, scorching their pristine Le Creuset cookware, all for the sake of obtaining holy, hole-y, and crispy-crust breads just like the ones you can get at a corner boulangerie in Paris.

If you're still not convinced of the impact of this revolutionary recipe, consider this. Googling the exact term "no-knead bread" will give you more than 100,000 links, while the shorter term "no-knead" results in nearly one-third more again. Home cooks were exploding the knob of their Le Creuset cookware pot lid, which are made to withstand only up to 375°F/190°C/Gas Mark 5 while the recipe calls for 450 to 500°F (230 to 260°C /Gas Mark 8 to 10), at the rate so alarming that replacements were reportedly sold out for a time. The crisis was so severe that cookware outlets complained of the mysterious disappearance of those knobs from their Le Creuset pots on display. The no-knead bread trend had turned otherwise innocent home cooks into petty thieves!

It took me awhile before I jumped onto this bandwagon. At first, I was unconvinced by the no-knead method. My Parisien friend David Lebovitz made have reportedly attained bread from the recipe that was less than satisfactory, though it looked perfect. In short, it seemed to be Hollywood bread: all the glitz and the glamour but no soul! But then I changed my mind.

It took an article by Jeffrey Steingarten in *Vogue* magazine to get me to sit up and pay attention. I know few other foodies with his level of compulsive obsession over even the most utterly minute details of the things he loves to eat. I read his treatise and decided if it's good enough for Jeffrey, I would give it a try.

So I set about making my first loaf following Jeffrey's recipe to the letter. There are few differences between that recipe and the original one published in the *New York Times*. Jeffrey's uses more salt and more yeast, and bakes his bread in a hotter oven, preferring 500°F/260°C/Gas Mark 10 rather than the 450°F/230°C/Gas Mark 8 specified in the original. Jeffrey's recipe also specified particular brands of bread flour and yeast, two of the three main components of the bread. I expected no less of him.

The result? Immediate success: gorgeous, irregular holes, super-crisp crust, and even holding its shape pretty well despite having started off as such a sticky, messy lump of dough. The bottom burnt a little, but I brushed it off as the simple mistake of a novice. I sure was one of those who'd never thought of making bread before.

The problem? No flavor! It tastes inoffensive and has a great texture and structure. Certainly, it was better than pretty much anything I could buy at the so-called bakeries near me. (But that's not really a big compliment given that I baked that first loaf in my kitchen in Santa Cruz, a town so sorely lacking in even remotely decent bread.)

All considered, I continued to bake the no-knead bread to fulfill my bread needs while in Santa Cruz. As soon as I arrived up in San Francisco I'd run straight to the 4 p.m. line at Tartine, or on a Saturday I'd be jostling the crowd in front of Edmund's Della Fattoria, or any day of the week at Bay Bread in Pacific Heights or Acme at the Ferry Plaza. Meanwhile, I kept experimenting with the recipe, searching for a way to put more flavor into my gorgeous no-knead loaves. I resisted using herbs, dried fruits, olives, or any of the usual additions to the bread. I wanted to put flavor into the bread itself, not to dress up the otherwise homely loaf in the culinary equivalent of bling.

HOW TO BE A FABULOUS FOODIE

I even baked a loaf in psychedelic purple. I had tasted *pain au vin* at Laurent Manrique's Gascogne restaurant, Fifth Floor; it was so great I decided to try to replicate it at home with a variant on the standard no-knead recipe. I replaced most of the water in the recipe with wine, which I had cooked down to get rid of most of the alcohol. The result didn't taste bad either. However, it is such an alarming shade of purple that it wasn't exactly appetizing.

My friend, avid amateur baker Robert Schonfeld, suggested I dump the yeast and instead use a sourdough starter. I was a little skeptical at first because what I've read in books and on the Internet about keeping and feeding a sourdough starter scares me a bit. All the calculation and daily feeding and making sure it doubles in volume and whatnot just seemed so complicated. One of the biggest advantages of the no-knead bread is that it involves little effort and you can whip it up whenever you want. The trouble with keeping alive a starter would eradicate that advantage.

The thought of trying a starter never really left me, however. One day, while having dinner at one of my favourite Santa Cruz hangouts, La Posta, the chef, Chris Avila, came out to chat. Chris had worked for David in the kitchen at Manresa years ago, so I knew him well. Chris bakes his own bread for the restaurant, and has a batch of 20-year-old starter bubbling in his walk-in refrigerator. He kindly offered to give me some to experiment on. I happily accepted.

So I took some of Chris's lively starter home. I experimented with a few combinations of flour, and ended up with a simple recipe of ⅓ cup/100g starter, ¾ cup/100g strong flour, and ¾ cup/100g water. I keep my starter in the fridge and feed it only a couple of times a week. To feed, I discard all but ⅓ cup/100g of the starter, then mix in ¾ cup/100g of strong flour and ¾ cup/100g of water until well-blended. I usually leave the freshly fed starter on the counter for a few hours to encourage it to grow before putting into the fridge to store.

Make sure you feed the starter the day you want to make bread. It takes about 8 hours for it to be most lively and ready for the dough. I usually bake bread in the morning, so I set my feeding regime in the morning to have the starter ready to be made into dough before I go to bed, as the no-knead bread will need to rest overnight (10 to 12 hours) before baking. If you want to bake bread in the evening instead, just switch your feeding regimen to every evening, then you can make your dough in the morning and have it ready to go in the oven around dinner time. It really is much simpler than it sounds, just a matter of setting a schedule that's convenient for you.

Robert helped adjust the ratio in the original no-knead recipe using commercial yeast into one using starter I now have in my pantry. I tried a number of four blend and end up with this one I love most, with a bit of spelt, barley, and wholewheat flour. It makes an absolutely delicious country loaf, slightly sour, not too dense, and with a very pleasantly nutty note.

14½oz | 410g flour blend, such as:
    6oz | 175g strong white flour
    3oz | 75g spelt
    3oz | 75g barley flour
    2½oz | 60g wholewheat flour

2 teaspoons (about 10g) kosher salt
8oz | 225g starter
8oz | 225g water (yes, weigh it!)
1 tablespoon honey

EQUIPMENT: *A 6 quarts/5.4 liter round pot*

Pour the flour blend into a large mixing bowl. You can use the blend I suggested here, or just make up your own, but I suggest you keep the strong white flour at the same amount and vary the quantity or type of other flours to get the flavor you want. I find that using a smaller ratio of strong white flour can turn the bread a little too dense for my taste. (Then again if that's what you are after, by all means, go with it.) Add the salt and mix well to incorporate it into the flour.

Add the starter, water, and honey. Mix everything until it comes together into a wet, well-incorporated lump of dough. Cover the bowl with plastic wrap and let it rest in a draft-free place for at least 12 hours.

Scrape the dough from the bowl onto a generously floured work surface. Pull the dough into a long rectangular shape. Pick up one end and fold one-third of it away from you, then pick up the other end and fold it over the first fold toward you to form a neat packet. Turn the dough packet around by 90 degrees and then stretch and fold it one more time in the same way.

Arrange the folded dough so that it is seam-side down on the work surface. Cover it with a kitchen towel and then an upturned bowl. You want to create a moist, closed environment. Leave the dough to rise for 2 hours.

After about 90 minutes, place the pot you plan to use to bake your bread with into the oven and turn it on to preheat to 450°F/230°C/ Gas Mark 8. If your kitchen is a little cool you can place the resting dough on top of the oven while it is heating up, which will help the dough rise a bit better.

When the oven is ready and the dough has rested for a full 2 hours, put on some oven mitts and remove the pot, which will be white hot, from the oven. The dough should be sturdy enough for you to pick up with two hands. Lift it into the pot, seam-side up, replace the lid, and put the pot back into the oven.

Bake the bread in the covered pot for 30 minutes, then remove the lid, and continue to bake for another 15 to 25 minutes or until the bread is golden brown. Remove the bread from the pot by tipping it upside down or you can lift it out with two wooden spoons, and let it cool on a wire rack. You should hear the bread crackle as it cools. This is a mixed-flour loaf, so it will look a bit denser than an all-white loaf would be.

Epilogue

Somehow, we've reached the end of this book, but, at risk of being ever-so-clichéd, this is merely the beginning. We began the journey in this book together by rediscovering our love of food. Along the way, we chatted about eating out, cooking in, drinking away our cares and, above all, we had a lot of fun. This isn't a conventional cook book. Some recipes are simplicity itself, while others are like that 1,500-word tome on the perfect Pad Thai. But that's life, no? Sometimes it's easy, other times, not so much. Either way, the important thing is that we are having a fabulous time.

I didn't set out to write the definitive guide on how to be a foodie, hence the "almost" in parentheses in the subtitle. How could it possibly be definitive when another chapter of my foodie life writes itself each day. There are always more bottles of wine to open, more books and blogs to read, more dishes to learn, and, yes, more restaurants to try. At a recent dinner party, my friend Annisa Helou gave me a handmade sieve for making couscous, and the very generous Paula Wolfert promised to teach me how to hand-roll them. I'm going to get around to taking Paula up on her offer very soon. And though I ran out of pages in this book to write about that experience, I'll certainly be documenting it on my blog, Chez Pim, for you to read.

Another chapter in your foodie life begins each day too, I'm sure. There's that new restaurant you've been meaning to try. That new blog you just added to your RSS reader. That new book Jeffrey Steingarten just published you've got to read. Oh, yes, and that mildly daunting Pad Thai recipe in this book you really should do one day soon. Happy eating!

I see you have a glass of wine in your hand too, so here's to our foodie life. *Salut!*

Index

First published in the United States of America in 2009 by
Chronicle Books LLC.
First published in England in 2009 by Conran Octopus Limited,
a part of Octopus Publishing Group.

Library of Congress Cataloging-in-Publication Data available.

ISBN 978-0-8118-6853-2

Manufactured in China.

Publisher: Lorraine Dickey
Managing Editor: Sybella Marlow
Art Direction and Design: Jonathan Christie
Color Photography: Pim Techamuanvivit
Black & White Photography: Jenny Acheson
Production Manager: Katherine Hockley

10 9 8 7 6 5 4 3 2 1

Chronicle Books LLC
680 Second Street
San Francisco, California 94107
www.chroniclebooks.com

pages 6–7: Strawberries in hibiscus and vanilla soup (page 20)